Advance praise for

MAKING A LIVING WHILE
MAKING A DIFFERENCE

Possibly the most visionary and integrated body of work in career development literature today.... Melissa Everett has made an enormous contribution to the field.

—Ande Diaz, author,
The Harvard College Guide to Careers in Public Service,
and Assistant Dean for Student Life, Princeton University

Melissa Everett is a unique career advisor. If I could have only one book for my career library, this would be it.

— Kevin Doyle, editor of
The Complete Guide to Environmental Careers in the 21st Century

For soul-satisfying adventure into Right Livelihood, Melissa Everett is the best guide around. In this savvy and exuberant book, she shows us how we can craft our work so that we can follow our heart's desire — to take part in the healing of our world. Must-reading for counselors, teachers, clergy, and all of us who want to come alive to the promise of our time.

—Joanna Macy, author, *Coming Back to Life*

Melissa Everett has given life and meaning and *access* to holistic work.

— Elly Jackson, co-author, *The New Perfect Resume*

We have entered a time when reinventing the world is front and center. Melissa Everett has written the operating instructions for working and thriving in this new economy. The potential for amazing jobs is unlimited. Read and learn how to partake of this bounty of contribution and financial reward.

— David Gershon, author,
Low Carbon Diet: 30 Day Program to Lose 5,000 Pounds and
Empowerment: The Art of Creating Your Life As You Want It

A highly useful and clearly thought out guide! This is an intriguing book that will lead you on the path to finding out what it is that you care deeply about, what feeds your soul, challenges your inner self, and brings meaning and peace to your life. As if that is not enough, Melissa helps you understand how you, a unique individual, can take control and create a purposeful lifestyle that truly will make a difference – in your life, the lives of others, the world around you – and pay the bills to boot!

— Ann Songyallo, Program Coordinator,
Department of Continuing and Professional Education,
SUNY Ulster

You probably picked up this book because you want your life to reflect your faith/values/politics/commitments/hopes/dreams/call. If you have arrived at a place where you know you want "more than just a job" or you want to think carefully about your life-purpose, this book is for you. This book is for you if you care about the world, people and/or yourself.

— Della Stanley-Green, Executive Director of
Indiana Network for Higher Education Ministries and
Project Director for Visions for Vocation.

MAKING A LIVING WHILE
MAKING A DIFFERENCE

REVISED EDITION
Conscious Careers for an Era of Interdependence

Melissa Everett

NEW SOCIETY PUBLISHERS

Cataloging in Publication Data:
A catalog record for this publication is available from the National Library of Canada.

Cover design by Diane McIntosh. Photos: iStock.

Printed in Canada. First printing October 2007.

Paperback ISBN: 978-0-86571-591-2

Inquiries regarding requests to reprint all or part of *Making a Living While Making a Difference* should be addressed to New Society Publishers at the address below.

To order directly from the publishers, please call toll-free
(North America) 1-800-567-6772, or order online at www.newsociety.com

Any other inquiries can be directed by mail to:

New Society Publishers
P.O. Box 189, Gabriola Island, BC V0R 1X0, Canada
(250) 247-9737

New Society Publishers' mission is to publish books that contribute in fundamental ways to building an ecologically sustainable and just society, and to do so with the least possible impact on the environment, in a manner that models this vision. We are committed to doing this not just through education, but through action. This book is one step toward ending global deforestation and climate change. It is printed on acid-free paper that is **100% post-consumer recycled** (100% old growth forest-free), processed chlorine free, and printed with vegetable-based, low-VOC inks, with covers produced using Forest Stewardship Council-certified stock. Additionally, New Society purchases carbon offsets based on an annual emissions audit, operating with a carbon-neutral footprint. For further information, or to browse our full list of books and purchase securely, visit our website at: www.newsociety.com

NEW SOCIETY PUBLISHERS   www.newsociety.com

To laugh often and love much;
to win the respect of intelligent people and the affection of children;
to earn the appreciation of honest critics
and endure the betrayal of false friends;
to appreciate beauty, to find the best in others;
to leave the world a bit better, whether by a healthy child,
a garden patch, or a redeemed social condition;
to know even one life has breathed easier because you have lived.
This is to have succeeded.

RALPH WALDO EMERSON

Never in my 25 years of leadership training
has there been a time when principles and pragmatism
have converged as completely as they do today.

STEVEN COVEY

There are at least two kinds of games.
One could be called finite, the other infinite.
A finite game is played for the purpose of winning,
an infinite game for the purpose of continuing the play...
Finite players play within boundaries;
infinite players play with boundaries.
Finite players are serious; infinite games are playful.
A finite player plays to be powerful;
an infinite player plays with strength.
A finite player consumes time;
an infinite player generates time.
The finite player aims for eternal life;
the infinite player aims for eternal birth.

JAMES CARSE, *FINITE AND INFINITE GAMES*

CONTENTS

ACKNOWLEDGMENTS

Let me express my heartfelt appreciation to the tribe of friends and colleagues, clients and strangers who have helped me bring this book to life by sharing their stories, resources and observations; reviewing chapters and testing exercises; challenging assumptions; and encouraging me to stay with the process. This has been a team project in all the best ways.

Personal thanks to networker and inspiration Matt Nicodemus for having the original idea for *Making a Living While Making a Difference* — at first "a little booklet" — and for being so good at getting other people to write books.

Special thanks to my agent, Tim Seldes, and the fabulous team at New Society Publishers.

Thanks to family, colleagues and friends, for handling the usual stresses with more than the usual grace.

The errors are all mine, of course. With this third, substantially rewritten, edition, hopefully they will be fewer.

Melissa Everett
Kingston, NY
melissae@earthlink.net

The Impact Factor

In today's wildly uncertain world of work, there is one thing above all that gives your career stability and coherence. That one thing makes you marketable in a completely distinctive way. That thing is your personal purpose and the impact you can have in the world — when you know these and take them seriously.

What about skills? They matter greatly. Cultivate them. Learn how to show them off with generosity.

What about your personality and your style — those intangibles that have given rise to such lucrative testing and typing industries? They matter — but maybe not as much as we tend to think. When you awaken your sense of purpose and let that become an organizing principle for your career, guess what? You'll bring forth new sides of yourself that you may never have thought possible.

What about your values? That is, what you view as good and right. Important, of course.

But look deeper into your own sense of what matters in the world — the work to be done that is bigger than anybody's personal career, the work that you would be most satisfied to be a part of. This isn't just a matter of what you hold as good and right in theory, but about what you *want* to see, for yourself and everyone you love. It's the package that holds values and desires. It's "where your great passion and the world's great hungers meet" — an axiom of career development coined a generation ago by Rev. Frederick Buechner. But "work with passion" has been trivialized, in many cases, by career guides that suggest you can have it all, that visualizing will make it so and that all passions are created equal. In conventional career-speak, you may have a passion for fashion, or for customer service, or for working in a bustling downtown office. As I'll use the term, however, passion comes in when you believe in these activities and projects as more than just a source of personal satisfaction — when you see them as important outside yourself. If you're really passionate about fashion, you'll be engaged in helping the industry do its work more responsibly and effectively for the long-term good. You may want to learn all about nontoxic dyes that don't harm textile workers, or promote organic fibers that don't deplete groundwater with excessive irrigation needs, or make sure the models aren't anorexic. You'll do it your way, by your values, but — as the term is used in these pages — passion is *somehow* larger than one person's life.

I'm a career counselor. I also run a regional organization focused on building an economy that benefits community and environment, with the humble name and mission of Sustainable Hudson Valley. On the side, I've been teaching in a technological university, helping young people develop their leadership skills and carry out service projects in the community. From where I sit, it seems that most people want to do something distinctive in their work and leave some legacy:

There's my friend Stacie, who works in her family's restaurant and spends her own time finding ways to increase local and organic food sourcing.

There's my old friend Gene, a "typical" hospital employee who spends all his "free" time working on clean elections and enlivens both of his worlds using his third skill set as a karaoke producer.

There's my friend Shirley, a "typical" social worker who is serious about helping people break out of dependency on social services and become culturally and economically empowered — so serious that she has created an exchange relationship between her New York colleagues and their counterparts in Africa and leads annual professional exchange tours to share new strategies for empowerment.

There's my landlord, Henry, a "typical" computer programmer who spends lots of free time as volunteer webmaster for avant garde art, radio and environmental groups' websites to help under-funded creative organizations get traction.

These people have figured out a key principle of surviving and thriving. The kinds of impact that you can create — at work, and more broadly in your life — are what make you valuable in the most distinctive way. Matching this "impact factor" with the workplaces that need what you have — whether they are many or few — connects you with the work opportunities where you will genuinely fit and thrive. This strategy anchors you in the industries, sectors, communities and subcultures that hold your best opportunities.

The Impact Factor draws together the conventional concerns of career assessment and planning — skills, personality, values. It does this in a way that moves the exploration from static to dynamic, that puts the pieces together into a more coherent pattern. This book will structure that exploration to address a number of "simple" questions — in depth.

The Impact Factor guides what you choose to do and how you choose to do it. You may be engaged in a fairly simple enterprise and yet put your distinct stamp on it by the values that guide your work and the choices you make on the path. For example, Jim Buckmaster, the CEO of CraigsList — a high-value company by any measure — floored Wall Street analysts in 2006 by announcing that he had no intention of trying to raise more money than needed to cover expenses, let alone maximize profit for shareholders.

These questions of guiding values have to do with a journey that most of us are on, a journey of relationships with our communities and the planet we live on. It is a journey through moment-to-moment choices about how to meet goals and expectations, avoid errors and have a positive impact. Sometimes these are subtle, and this book aims to draw them out. Sometimes they have the potential to be dramatic, and this book is an invitation to accept authentic drama when it comes to call.

The first edition of this book was published in 1995, when a few realities were just dawning on the culture and the career pundits. We were just coming to terms with the degree of loss of manufacturing jobs — and even service jobs — through outsourcing offshore and the globalization of the economy. The direction of the economy, and the ways to make a living within it, were radically unknown. Since then, at least in my view, a number of trends have come into focus that clarify the picture:

Success habits. Many more people know the basics of networking, telling their story, finding opportunities and negotiating deals. A lot have also done some basic work on themselves to step out of limiting attitudes, take responsibility for their own growth, handle conflict and tap their own inner power. This edition starts with the assumption that readers get it and are on the path.

Open source. As information proliferates and people learn the value of sharing it, a new work ethic is coming into play that rewards open communication more than hoarding resources. This means the mutual self-help approach that's outlined in these pages is better understood than it once was — though it still hasn't taken hold everywhere.

Entrepreneurship. Small, independent business is making a comeback with a vengeance and a vision — as a positive force in our communities by keeping dollars recirculating and doing business with community and environment in mind. The Business Alliance for Local Living Economies (livingeconomies .org) and the American Independent Business Alliance (amiba.org) have helped to bring this vision to life in scores of communities, side by side with local business groups; this movement is growing fast. Sustainable Business Alliances are actively educating consumers on the benefits of buying local and on green building and living. Many people have been self-employed, and even more appreciate the value of an entrepreneurial attitude, no less in government and nonprofits than in business.

Sustainability. Fewer and fewer people think it is possible to succeed in business without succeeding in a broader way, by creating work organizations that do not burn out or abuse employees; that treat customers honestly; engage with communities in a positive way; and preserve and restore the natural environment. In nutshell, this is the concept of sustainable economic development. The necessity and possibility for a breakthrough into sustainable forms of economic development is a guiding premise of this book. As director of an organization that is working on it for an important region, New York's Hudson River Valley, I am more hopeful every day.

In a sustainable economy, what would the work look like? Here is one vision, resulting from a focused exploration by some 50 organizations, the North American Consultation on Sustainable Livelihoods, convened to wrestle with this question back in the 1990s. These guiding principles are still on track today. They may not be fully reflected in any job, but they are relevant to each and every job and business opportunity.

"Sustainable livelihoods provide meaningful work that fulfills the social, economic, cultural and spiritual needs of all members of a community — human, non-human, present and future — and safeguards cultural and biological diversity."[1] Therefore these approaches to work tend to:

• Promote equity between and among generations, races, genders and ethnic groups; in the access to and distribution of wealth and resources; in the sharing of productive and reproductive roles; and the transfer of knowledge and skills.

• Nurture a sense of place and connection to the local community and adapt to and restore regional ecosystems.

- Stimulate local investment in the community and help to retain capital within the local economy.
- Base production on renewable energy and on regenerating local resource endowments while reducing intensity of energy use, eliminating overconsumption of local and global resources and assuring no net loss of biodiversity.
- Utilize appropriate technology that is ecologically fitting, socially just and humane, and that enhances rather than displaces community knowledge and skills.
- Reduce as much as possible travel to the workplace and distance between producers and users.
- Generate social as well as economic returns and value nonmonetized as well as paid work.
- Provide secure access to opportunity and meaningful activity in community life.

The goal of this book is to help you seek out opportunities to achieve as many of these visions as possible, while meeting your own needs for income, satisfaction and growth. I call this approach "*Self*-employment" — that is, bringing your "big self" to work, the self that is in touch with your power and empathy. This book is for you if you want to make a difference in your world — whether your world is a classroom, a neighborhood or the planet. Most people, at some level, do want exactly this — if they give themselves permission to notice the desire. It's common to think that we can only aspire to an impact in the wider world after we have met our basic needs and sorted out our identity. Abraham Maslow's famous "hierarchy of needs" proposed viewing human development this way. But later psychological theory and practice has complicated the story in a very useful manner, by suggesting that, in fact, we can better take care of our basics and work out our identity by the act of connecting with the wider world. Our identity and vocation — that is, calling — is only revealed through connections, and that means through experience. Four social psychologists — Larry Daloz-Parks, Sharon Parks-Daloz, Jim and Cheryl Keen — studied the "lives of commitment" of 100 effective professionals working for a better world in successful careers.[2] They found, as a guiding principle of these people's development, an opening up of caring and compassion without an ability to predict results. That act of choice was what made creativity flow and, in some cases, actually created opportunities. What is more, the four authors carried out over 100 structured interviews over several years, as a team, and finished the project with marriages and friendships in tact. Their work in bringing these stories of commitment to light also reflects lives of commitment.

This book will guide you through a process of vocational self-discovery and career development that is simple but not easy. It provides basic yet thorough guidance in every phase of the process, from self-assessment and goal setting through investigating the options, preparing your résumé and other marketing materials, applying and campaigning for jobs or starting and building a business. It carries forward one more step beyond securing the next opportunity — to identify an approach to ongoing career development as a "co-creator" of the workplace you want.

- You will begin simply by paying attention — real attention — to what you most care about. What issues attract or repel you in the news? Whose work fascinates you in your own social networks?

- Next, you will pause to get traction by stabilizing your life with regard to time, money, clutter and relationships — four dimensions of life that can strongly enable or inhibit your successful stepping out. This does not need to be a major campaign in itself — just a moment of marshalling resources and reducing distraction in order to move ahead with clarity.

- Next, this guidebook will help you to investigate the industries and occupations that attract you — with skills and strategies as well as essential resources.

- Then, it will structure your assessment of your own Impact Factor. It will work with the usual elements, including your core aptitudes and specialized skills, with your values, and also with unorthodox questions including your attitudes toward mobility and place, technology, money and beauty.

- Looking at these elements, together, you will focus on the essence of your work in the world and the next good ideas for translating it into job or business opportunities. You will be invited to make a commitment to those aspects of the path that are clear, and take action — whether as a volunteer or an entrepreneur — to begin creating your vision.

- Next is the search and/or business planning process, in a paradoxical pair of chapters: one about organizing, and the other about surrender.

- Finally, we will explore ways to refine your positioning and strategy within any job or business, conscious career development by co-creating your workplace and relationships.

Every guide is based on theories about the way the world works and where economy and society are headed. This guide is based on the notion that effective enterprises, in the long run, are the ones that are most self-aware and on purpose with regard to their social and environmental impact, and create value in diverse ways that build support for their core business in turn. Career sustainability comes from aligning your working life with the more sustainable, conscious, principled and accountable enterprises, whether in corporations, independent business, government or not-for-profit organizations. Because these organizations are less secretive, more effective at working in partnerships and alliances, better networked and often higher-profile, they are also better platforms for career moves and prominence in your field.

There is increasingly strong documentation of this point. Research by Innovest Strategic Value Advisors, ranking companies on environmental performance metrics and comparing these ranks with shareholder value, finds strong correlation year after year. Many studies echo this, and few dispute it. Now, sustainability is at the top of many CEOs' agendas, as reflected by the content of key global meetings like the World Economic Forum.[3] As a result, there has been a substantial growth and diversification of socially responsible investment funds — an estimated 20% of all assets under management in 2005, according to a Social Investment Forum study.[4]

Those who understand these connections may work in corporations, independent business, non-profits or government — or they may move among these sectors. Wherever, they reflect an emerging work ethic, one that connects their work for material sustenance with the work they each do to make their communities and natural surroundings more livable. In spite of the turbulence and uncertainty everywhere, they are builders. They naturally reach for opportunities to make positive changes in the world, from protecting and restoring the environment, to reducing violence and poverty, to making society's institutions work. They realize that all the volunteering in the world will not be enough to counter the impact of working lives that have not been designed to take either environmental or human well-being into account. So they are searching for effective ways to be part of redesigning the economy — one organization, one project, one career at a time. They want to devote their working lives to some kind of tangible, positive change. What drives them isn't a sense of duty or guilt, but a spirit of engagement and curiosity.

One major national study estimates that the population with these values is 50 million strong (as of 2000) or 26% of the population and calls them the

"Cultural Creatives."[5] What sets Cultural Creatives apart is a combination of environmental, social and spiritual values, all arising from the view of themselves as interconnected and interdependent with the world around them. For them, taking care of the environment and solving entrenched social problems are no longer fringe concerns but essentials. Work is not the only arena for this exploration, but it's a major one. This is a career guide for people who understand that our lives are substantially constructed by our surroundings and our choices and that we can't wait to inherit a future — we need to create one worthy of the effort.

This requires looking at the current state of the world — and the crying need for human initiative and effort — without diving under the bed. This, in turn, requires taking a look at the peculiar apathy that many of us experience when the conversation turns toward difficult ecological and social issues, from domestic violence to global terrorism. Research on the phenomenon of psychic numbing makes it clear that people do not shut down on big-picture issues out of a lack of caring. They shut down because they care too much, and it hurts too much sometimes to look at the mess we are in. It hurts, especially, when we feel powerless to act. Numbing and apathy are directly proportional to the perception of powerlessness. And they deepen that sense of powerlessness by cutting us off from our lighter feelings as well as those of despair. Holding our concerns for the world around us at bay and trying to behave "normally," we begin to feel fraudulent if not crazy. We lose our sense of inner authority.

The antidote to all this is a cluster of very distinctive learning experiences that pulls us out of isolation, lets us feel and speak our own truths about the state of the world and the work that needs doing, allows our voices to be heard to restore our faith in our own perceptions and then turns attention toward the creativity that is released after repressed emotions are let out. This happens, for example, through:

- Learning to pay attention to the world with multiple intelligences: emotional, kinesthetic, visual, imaginative and so on, as well as analytical.
- Developing fresher, more subtle perceptions of the world and the work to be done in it, and using them to challenge perceived limits about our choices.
- Cultivating a sense of personal power by doing what we can do and building a support system.
- Creating and celebrating beauty, in every possible form, to keep us animated.

Only by opening up, in these ways, to the full spectrum of experience can we rise to the immense challenge of organizing our working lives with our communities and the Earth firmly in mind. Only then can we do the right things, not as a "should," but out of recognition of the enlightened self-interest of preserving our social and ecological life-support system. As Norwegian philosopher Arne Naess puts it, "When the social self is well developed, and I understand that I am part of something larger, I no longer want to eat a big cake all by myself. I want to share it with others."[6] So, too, with finding ways to earn livelihoods that maximize benefit to the world around us, as well as being personally satisfying. In keeping with good ecological thinking, *Making a Living While Making a Difference* stresses everybody's right and need to adapt these principles to their own circumstances. Above all, it's about freeing up more of our true Selves and bringing them to bear in the work we do. As examples will show, the rewards can put the risks in an entirely different perspective.

Career decision-making today is more complicated than the road maps will ever be. We are not only deciding among more options than ever; we are deciding how to decide. What's real? What's essential? What work will make a difference? What institutions are capable of doing it? Where do we place our trust? With respected businesses that show solid increases in stock value? With nonprofits whose mission statements are really compelling? With public agencies that have gotten serious about reinventing government and are embarked on fascinating experiments in new ways to serve the public? With charismatic leaders? With organizations that show results we care about, or the ones whose cultures and day-to-day operating principles seem most wholesome?

With the guiding structure of a ten step program, *Making a Living While Making a Difference* approaches life/work planning in several distinctive ways:

- It focuses on having enough and creating a satisfying life, not on having it all.
- It goes beyond the notion of utilitarian networking to encourage the creation of real community around us, not only when it is useful for a transition, but to feed us and give back.
- It views career development within a web of stakeholders who are touched by our choices — from up-close ones like family and co-workers, out to the communities and natural environments our choices affect.
- It takes an entrepreneurial view for everyone, whether an employee or business owner, and whether you are in the private sector, government or nonprofits.

- It works with a paradoxical pair of strategies for advancing your career: commitment and surrender.

"Self-employment," then, is not just about finding or creating work that helps rebuild communities and the planet, although that is sorely needed. It isn't simply the ability to get paid to do something fascinating. It's work that links external contribution with personal development and satisfaction in the way that is right for you.

When we're contemplating a choice, many of us focus on the risks. How different the same choice can look from the other side, when we can also see the possible gains, and the inner resources we free up by acting on our true values. One of the courageous clients and workshop participants who remind me of this is Peter. He was hooked by an idea that had taken over his imagination, but he couldn't figure out how to activate it. He wanted to create an ecological retreat center with demonstration organic gardens, green building practices, meeting spaces and many other features. One inner voice told him it was a crazy notion. Another voice told him it was his future. Throughout a workshop, his questions were all about the costs of taking the plunge: reduced earnings, compromised credibility, his wife's uncertainties. Finally, I asked him, "How do you know this idea would be so impractical? How do you know you would earn less than you do now? Have you done a business plan? Have you done market research?"

"No. I've been too scared. I really have no idea," he replied. Just a few months later, Peter sent me a beautiful brochure for the new center, with the next season's program and a note of thanks.

You cannot control the economy or the course of planetary civilization. But you can very much control your responses to it and your stance within it. Taking personal responsibility for those choices is a key to getting your career aligned with your own values and pictures of reality and with emerging opportunities. This is the most genuine form of job security in the world today. Whatever risks and opportunities you are dancing with, I hope this book will provide a tangible support for breaking out of perceived limits and stepping into a future worthy of your commitment.

PART ONE

THE WORK TO BE DONE

CHAPTER 1

Organizing the Infinite: Fields of Opportunity

The work opportunities available today represent a dazzling range in quality, content and compensation. There is no one way to organize your exploration of them. In fact, this chapter suggests several and offers you the orientation that will help you to engage effectively with the Ten Step Program. We will look at some ways to sort out the kinds of organization you might work in (or create), the industries and occupations you might step into and, finally, some clusters of occupations and industries that represent especially important areas of opportunity for making a living and a difference.

Four Sectors

I believe there are four distinct kinds of workplace in today's economy, based on their ownership structure, how they are controlled and the incentives and constraints that guide their operations. Each of these is actually a different arena of opportunity and risk for the job seeker:

- Corporate, for-profit business
- Independent, for-profit business
- Non-profit, public-interest organizations including charities, trade associations, unions and faith communities
- Government at all scales, from local to global

There are also intriguing hybrid forms emerging, including the "B corporation" or "for-benefit" private business that is organized to generate profit but contains in its charter a commitment to environmentally and/or socially responsible practices with formal accounting of impacts. These are a minute fraction of the economy, but certainly of interest to the entrepreneur.

3

Every sector has some great organizations and opportunities. Every sector is diverse. But each of these kinds of workplace has characteristics that define how it legally has to work and that tend both to reflect its culture and to shape it.

A **public corporation**, owned by shareholders, is commonly set up and operated as a system for maximizing efficiencies and generating substantial profits on investment — whether or not profits are "maximized," a tough concept to define in any event. Corporations are chartered for limited liability to those shareholders in order to deal with risks, and this sits at the core of controversy about the corporation's social responsibility. Many corporations are guided by economies of scale and geographic flexibility, and can move around the globe to follow the availability of capital, markets and resources. Because a corporation is owned by shareholders and legally answerable to them — and because corporations have been so heavily scrutinized through the scandals of recent years — corporate employers tend to:

- Have clearly spelled out policies and procedures;
- Achieve economic advantage by centralizing key operations like training and purchasing, which can limit the diversity possible in local operations;
- Have access through their national and international networks to financial and training resources not always easily available to more local, smaller-scale businesses;
- Value consistency and coordination — think "branding" — even as they may genuinely wrestle with ways to empower and reward employees.

Shareholder-owned corporations are not all massive or devoid of vision. Nau, the first corporation officially chartered to follow a "multiple-bottom-line" business model, arose in 2007. And there is increasing experimentation with new forms of stock issuance to close the gap between risk management and values orientation. A great example is the Mercantile, a community-owned retail store in Powell, Wyoming. When the tiny town lost its department store and could not attract a retail chain, a small group of citizens organized the creation of a community-owned retail store, selling shares for $500 and carrying a good range of national brands.

Since the serious corporate accountability scandals of the late 1990s — in which Enron, WorldComm, Arthur Andersen and others brought down shareholders, pension funds, employees and to a certain extent regional economies — corporate practice has been more highly regulated and has in many cases become more transparent, opening up more space for innovation. The Global Reporting Initiative, a common form and platform for corporate environmental reporting, had nearly 2,000 company reports in its registry by early 2007.[1]

An **independent business** is privately owned by an individual or small group without selling stock and without limited liability. Independent businesses may also grow quite large, but most have to open up ownership to additional investors or sell shares to reach national or global scale. In the last few years, a vibrant movement of independent businesses has arisen with a focused social mission and strategy — to remain small and grow by deepening roots in communities rather than by broadening influence. Organizations including the American Independent Business Alliance (amiba.net) and the Business Alliance for Local Living Economies (livingeconomies.org) are fast-growing networks of these businesses, modeling community benefit and attracting community support for the businesses through "local first" consumer education campaigns and market development projects. Independent businesses may be very well capitalized and reach significance in a region; they may even establish chains and franchises. What sets them apart is their ability to make decisions, within the law but without the control of shareholders who may be motivated either to maximize profit or minimize risk. Co-Op America suggests that a healthy community ought to have a particular list of independent businesses thriving within it, offering opportunities in case yours does not. For example, does your hometown have, or need, a locally owned:

- Grocery
- Child Care Center
- Newspaper
- Cleaning Service
- Builders' Supply
- Car Repair
- Bed and Breakfast
- "Wet" cleaner or non-toxic dry cleaner
- Restaurant
- Body Care Shop
- Clothing Shop
- General Store
- Lawn Care Service
- Bicycle Shop
- Bank

Not all independent businesses are community-friendly, but — when they aren't — their owners are likely to be more accessible than those of a public corporation.

Small and even tiny businesses can influence big ones in several ways. For example, as consultants they can bring essential expertise and knowledge into the mix. Green Order, a startup consultancy, is credited with helping to create the world-famous EcoMagination program for creating greener products in one of the most prominent corporations, General Electric. Small companies can also influence large ones as suppliers by bringing them better or more distinctive products. Where I live, a tiny company called Hudson Valley Fresh has the ambitious goal of changing the economics of the dairy industry to get farmers a living wage for their products. CEO Sam Simon, a retired MD, is doing this by producing high-end whole and chocolate milk with a less depressed price than the industry as a whole receives and marketing it in affluent communities as the gourmet product he knows it is.

Non-profit organizations are named confusingly, since they are perfectly able to make a profit — even a substantial one. What they cannot do is return profits to shareholders. Instead, those profits go back into the organization to further its chartered mission, which might be to expand literacy in a community or to defend the rights of a neighborhood that has been dumped on with toxic wastes. Non-profits, fundamentally, are organizations driven by a mission. That mission may be complex. The organization may be facing tough dilemmas about how to advance it. There may not be a paying market — for example, if the organization is focused on alleviating poverty. With special tax status to allow financing through donations, memberships, grants — and often contracts and modest profit streams as well — non-profit institutions are a varied and essential component of the economy and especially the "innovation sector." Not just education and advocacy groups, but universities, unions and religious denominations are among the organizations that raise public support for a public purpose using non-profit status.

Despite stereotypes about low pay and chronic dysfunction — which in my experience are no more prevalent in non-profits than in the private and governmental sectors — non-profit organizations are an amenable home to many people working for social or environmental change. According to the *Non-profit Times* 2005 survey of salaries and working conditions, CEO salaries average around $90,000 per year, reflecting the enormous range between highly paid college and hospital presidents and struggling heads of community development or literacy programs.[2] Benefits packages are becoming competitive with the private sector, yet more subject to scrutiny. Professional vacations and educational expense coverage are common, bonuses and perks not related to work are more rare. *Non-profit Times* reports an "accordion-like expansion and contraction" of employment opportunities, as well as high regional variation, for a number of reasons, including a high proportion of campaign-oriented work with natural beginnings and ends, and ongoing experiments with technologies to replace complex human functions.

An enormous range of activity and impact comes from this sector. The work of charitably organized non-profits includes:

- Scientific research — for example, the Union of Concerned Scientists conducts independent reviews on climate science; the Metropolitan Conservation Alliance at the Bronx Zoo helps community planners to design streets and other infrastructure in ways that preserve wildlife migratory pathways.
- Creative arts — Lincoln Center is a non-profit employer, and your local Arts Council may be as well.
- Healthcare — even giant hospital systems may be organized as non-profits and may depend upon foundation grants, charitable gifts and fundraisers to support services for low-income clients.
- Setting standards for business — Social Accountability International is a non-profit that has created, and helps to implement, standards for workplace safety and human rights in international workplaces, especially for contractors to corporations that want to minimize risk and ensure legal compliance.

The "social sector" is also emerging as a "beta site" for developing and rigorously testing new products and service. As Rosabeth Kanter reports in *Harvard Business Review*:

> Today several leading companies are beginning to find inspiration in an unexpected place: the social sector — in public schools, welfare-to-work programs and the inner city. These companies have discovered that social problems are economic problems, whether it is the need for a trained workforce or the search for new markets in neglected parts of cities. They have learned that applying their energies to solving the chronic problems of the social sector powerfully stimulates their own business development. Today's better-educated children are tomorrow's knowledge workers. Lower unemployment in the inner city means higher consumption in the inner city. Indeed, a new paradigm for innovation is emerging: a partnership between private enterprise and public interest that produces profitable and sustainable change for both sides.[3]

Government is a major employer at every scale from village to global. The funding for government programs — and for government itself — is embattled in the current political climate, and waves of local government downsizing were taking place in several states as this book went to press. But government continues to perform essential functions and provide a fertile ground for innovation, through cycles of expansion and contraction.

Elected officials may be paid or volunteer. Professional and technical workers in government may run agencies — from education to finance to public works. They may be hired with "soft" money for special programs. And established positions, from mayor to public works commissioner, provide platforms for innovation, as over 500 municipalities showed by their participation in the US Mayors' Climate Protection Agreement.[4] Finally, consultants to government, though "outside" the civil service structure, may become well established in niches such as planning and education.

The federal government, most states and some counties employ a spectrum of professional and scientific staffs in areas such as public health, energy innovation and educational certification. Lawyers, scientists, policy and statistical analysts, information technology professionals and investigators are part of the essential workings of government. Needs for specialists abound — usually far outpacing funding for them. Even a generalist in government, like an elected official, will be tested for the ability to take in technical knowledge and make complex decisions on everything from water systems to immigration policy.

Working in governmental programs often involves a mix of enforcing law and policy and promoting positive behavior change by working closely with members of the community. People skills, and judgment, are paramount in governmental work, and all the more since most governments are struggling to manage partisan divisions and get things done. Especially when innovation is afoot, these jobs are heavy in community relations and marketing.

As long as policy innovation and bottom-line responsibility remain primarily at the local and state levels, more and more of the work to be done in implementing policies is there too: through elected officials, political appointees and their staffs and the wide range of technical assistance and advocacy organizations that work with them. More and more environmental protection decisions are being made at the local level, from the delivery of municipal services to land protection to transportation policy to industrial development decisions. As a result, local governments are employing recycling coordinators and market developers, bike trail developers, water conservation educators, planners and many other specialists. There might be fewer than half a dozen of these in a small town and a hundred in a major city. But with 17,000 cities, towns, counties and other local entities on the US map, the opportunities add up.

According to Dennis Church, who has helped design these programs for such cities as San José, California, "Local governments have always had a primary responsibility for environmental quality. They, after all, plan land use and transportation systems, adopt and enforce codes, run local water and sewer utilities, pick up the garbage and recycling and so on." He outlines three categories of local jobs: designing programs to meet these environmental goals — and keeping the municipality in compliance with federal and state regulations. The second is enforcing local law and policy. The third, and often most creative, is working proactively to help businesses, homeowners and others find greener ways to do what they do.

Government jobs can be local, state, federal, international and regional, as well as hybrids of these. Regional associations and councils of government are formed to address social or environmental problems that are larger than a community but do not fit neatly in state boundaries, such as air quality, immigration or trade. Many government jobs require a mix of technical, conceptual and political skills that doesn't come easy for everyone. For the same reasons they're challenging, though, they can provide a base for experimentation and a surprising degree of mobility. Church notes, "You have to have the communications skill and savvy to overcome the natural mistrust that may occur when you say, 'I'm from the government, and I'm here to help.'" No matter how much government may devolve, there will always be a large role for federal, state, regional and local agencies in implementing current policies and building the next generation's policy framework.

Jobs Our Parents Never Heard Of

It is hard to take in just how broad and diverse the economy is, and how bizarrely different the work opportunities are. Try talking about work on a visit to your parents — or, for that matter, your children. The waters you are swimming in may astonish others. You can be an underwater robotics specialist. A geriatric cosmetologist. An urban forester. A carbon trader. A cross-cultural mediator. Or the marketing director for a dating service. Let's look more closely, though, at some reasons why these opportunities are so diverse and at the broader trends we can learn more about to make the quest a little more co-herent. New industries and occupations are emerging because of:

New tools. In the last couple of generations, humans have got much more crafty with our tools and technologies, and some of these developments are to be celebrated. We can manipulate data at scales from parts per trillion to global trends, creating opportunities in technology in modeling, instrumentation, data management and representation (including fancy mapping), remote sensing and more.

New opportunities. Recognition of an issue that has awakened millions — global warming — combines with a new strategy for financing a response, namely, the trading of carbon credits, financially rewarding the virtuous and charging the rest. Trading systems work because they ultimately reduce the license to pollute over time, and increase the cost of doing so. Trading exchanges such as the Chicago Climate Exchange, and offset services such as DriveNeutral, are employers our parents never heard of in the climate protection world.

New needs. These might result from changing demographics, environmental conditions, policies or cultural values. A dating service is a social innovation to bring people together. A century ago, when communities were more stable, this happened through existing networks (and it still does, of course). An ecological restoration business is newly needed because modern development patterns have so degraded natural systems.

New scope. As people and capital move around the globe, new scopes are attached to existing jobs. International law and human rights, cross-cultural mediation or global logistics are jobs our parents definitely didn't have on the radar.

New markets/populations. People in need, and people with resources, are always targets for specialized industries. This translates, at a minimum, to specialty services and products for the very old, the very young, people with handicaps, people resettling from afar and/or speaking different languages, the fast-growing population in poverty and the growing number of millionaires. Seniors don't just need supports in maintaining quality of life, but at times in day-to-day support and self-defense (including lawyers specializing in scam protection).

New combinations. Farms and forests have been with us a long time. But agroforestry is a new specialty that helps integrate them, to allow for forest-floor cash crops (like ginseng) and for farm-based woodlots, as extra sources of cash and as ways toward more sophisticated, environmentally sound and financially viable land use.

Fields of Opportunity

While all this complexity is real, we will be better off looking beneath it for some broader guiding principles for uncovering good work. I am going to propose a simple set of three fundamental categories of work that makes a difference, and they correspond with addressing human and environmental needs at three scales: personal, community and planet.

Healthy basics. You walk into the supermarket and a luscious red apple catches your eye. It's locally grown. It's organic. And it's affordable. When this happens (or even two out of three of these victories), it is thanks to the work of a long and complex chain of people. The produce manager who made the selection in the store. The distributors and marketing people who built the bridge between orchard and store. The inspector in the state certification program who determined that the orchard land was fit for organic growing. The state assembly staffers who drafted the legislation for the certification program. The citizen activists who showed them the public support for doing it. The county extension agents who learned new Integrated Pest Management techniques to help farmers. The bankers who maintained farm-friendly credit practices. Oh, and of course, the farmers. An explosion of concern about personal health is going on, and environmental sources of illness are a major component. These range from sick buildings to unsafe drinking water to unhealthy personal care products to foods produced in ways that are hazardous to people or the environment. The natural foods industry is growing at annual rates between 10 percent and 20 percent, with natural food "stores" appearing under the roofs of many mega-supermarkets. This is taking place because large numbers of people are concerned and becoming educated about the food they put into their bodies. Major national food companies are developing their own organic product lines — for instance, yogurts from General Foods and Dannon — and buying up natural and organic food startups to enter these markets. This trend creates new jobs and alters the nature of others, including those in agriculture, distribution, marketing, regulation and agricultural products and services. And the growth of the natural food industry dovetails with a host of other trends that could be grouped together as "non-toxic living," from carpets without toxic glue to cosmetics without formaldehyde. Finding healthy ways of meeting basic human needs — food, shelter, personal care and health products — is an enormous emerging area for employment and business opportunity.

Livable communities. You are walking down to the corner café at dusk to buy a local newspaper, and you notice how pleasant it is to have a corner café and to be near it, rather than in traffic, and as the sun sets, how reassuring it is to feel safe strolling in your own neighborhood, since you remember years when the streets were less welcoming. Finally, you give thanks that there is a local paper available, owned by people you've met, to give you a flavor of news and commentary not available from the newspaper chains. "Livable communities" is an intentionally broad category — broad enough to represent the range of concerns that might be important to you, from safety to health to containment of sprawl so that residences and commerce are arranged for a mix of utility and beauty. The coalition of people and organizations working on some version of livability — sometimes marketed as Smart Growth — is enormous, and it reflects a wide spectrum of views on how much growth can be smart in the final analysis. New Jersey, Maryland and Minnesota are among the states that pioneered the establishment of offices of sustainable development, which are more and more widespread. You can work on creating more livable communities as an elected official or staffer, employee of a regulatory agency, architect, designer, landscaper, gardener, planner, manager of public or private lands, police and court employee working on violence prevention, banker and venture capitalist, local entrepreneur or staffer in a business association, labor representative, or advocate focusing on safer streets, housing, planning and zoning, employment issues, dispute resolution, public transportation and more.

Planet protection. While it may be harder to visualize concretely, global environmental challenges are also creating a large agenda for human labor to turn around a sobering situation.

The most discussed planetary crisis, as this book is completed, is the climate crisis. As businesses appreciate the financial risks of storms, droughts and other climate-related catastrophes, this crisis is translating directly into jobs and business opportunities. These begin with energy conservation and innovation in the broadest sense, including the development of new technologies and policies and the reorganization of our local and regional economies to reduce reliance on polluting transportation technologies. Most people may prefer not to think about energy when they're not flipping a switch or changing a fuse. But energy conservation, sustainable energy sources and production of materials with greatly improved energy efficiency are all cutting edges of our technological economy and are becoming comparative advantages for innovative regions including Silicon Valley, greater Boston and possibly New York's Hudson River corridor (where some of us are working on it as we speak). This means real work for engineers and technicians in solar, wind, biofuels, cogeneration, heat pumps, distributed energy systems, fuel cells and other energy technologies. Importantly, responding to global warming's almost-certain impacts, as well as fighting to reduce future climate change, also means protecting and enhancing water supply and water efficiency everywhere, giving rise to career paths in technology and also in landscape design and management. This set of challenges means roles for research and development groups in universities, industry and government; installation and repair technicians; marketing firms and venture capital companies; trade association staff people and union organizers; vice-presidents of marketing and sales managers; customer service representatives and quality assurance people; wholesalers and retailers — for these large companies and the thousands of entrepreneurial businesses that will sell to them, subcontract for them and, at times, compete with them. Even the simplest, no-brainer strategy for protecting climate, namely, energy efficiency and prudent use, is an arena for the marketing of products and for innovative businesses — energy service companies such as Efficiency Vermont — that helps businesses and homes to save energy and are paid through the streams of savings. These niches add up to a large and growing slice of the economy. This sector is increasingly known as CleanTech.[5] But the opportunities are broader still: to adapt the operations of every workplace by reducing greenhouse gas emissions as close as possible to zero so they do not impact negatively on global systems.

The global issue of protecting biological diversity and reducing pressures on habitats is a second example with enormous ramifications for the performance of our jobs, as well as business opportunities. There's work to be done by wildlife biologists and their support staffs; mapping and data management specialists; mathematicians; programmers; rangers and maintenance staff in parks and preserves; land trust professionals and support staff who negotiate and finance land purchases, then oversee wild lands in ways that are consistent with conservation goals; governmental planning departments and private consulting firms; attorneys, advocates and policy experts who understand the intricacies of the Endangered Species Act, international biodiversity convention and the like; environmental education and science museum staff who educate the public to build a consensus for conservation; resource economists who figure out how to place a fair dollar value on natural resources lost or preserved; environmental reporters who translate the global picture into locally meaningful terms; and more. There are also business opportunities in ecotourism, sustainable agriculture and forestry, natural pharmaceuticals and personal care products and financing strategies for land conservation. Finally, there is an enormous need for eco-literate managers, finance people, marketers, lawyers, product developers and community relations managers in all the organizations that occupy land and make decisions about its wise use — that is, throughout the economy.

Each of these fields of opportunity — healthy basics, livable communities and planet protection — crosscuts the four sectors of corporations, independent business, non-profits and government. One of the skills for effective career development is to move flexibly among the sectors to follow (or create) the opportunities. For example, sustainable development policies have long been advocated by non-profits working in legislation, standard-setting, education and public information. As possibilities have been uncovered, entrepreneurs have run with them and often refined the policy playing field in partnerships such as the Coalition for Environmentally Responsible Economies (CERES), a large investor coalition with participation from all sectors. The sustainable business sector, and its individual businesses, have matured through competition and partnership and have often worked in partnership with non-profits through their philanthropy. As ideas have flowed among the sectors, they have significantly influenced each other's practices and cultures. For many reasons, non-profits are rising to the responsibility of becoming more businesslike, in creating clear revenue models, budgeting and performance targets. Businesses are taking on some of the non-profit flair with greater self-expression and articulation of social and environmental missions. Government, interacting with them all, has opened up both to fiscal discipline and innovative possibility.

The next chapters will go into more detail on several clusters of industries that hold special opportunities for making a difference, as well as a living. Some are connected with benefit to humans, others with benefit to the natural environment. Many touch both.

CHAPTER 2

Work that Protects and Restores the Environment

Food and Forests

There is vigorous debate on what constitutes a healthy food system but increasing agreement about some things that stress it: overuse of pesticides, herbicides, preservatives, petrochemicals and water; too much distance between producer and consumer; irradiation and genetic modification of crops; unsustainable harvesting practices, whether depleting the ocean with overfishing or the fields with monoculture crops. The complex of businesses and public sector enterprises that works together to put the food on your table is vast and so are the opportunities to reduce the distance between farm and table, increase the safety of food and equity of access to it.

There are over 5,000 certified organic farms in the US. Farms tend to employ "multi-specialists" who can get crops to grow, fix the truck and design a marketing brochure — and they often have very part-time or intermittent work for people with one of those skill sets. Generalist or specialist, you can manage a farm designed to reflect your values and the strengths of your bioregion, from produce to specialty cash crops like medicinal herbs and gourmet goodies, as well as crops for fiber (like the paper substitute kenaf); for building materials (they're growing bamboo in Massachusetts!) and for fuel (like prairie grasses or willow for biofuels). The ecological sustainability of all these crops depends on location, scale, approach and what they might displace (like food). But as these new farm-based industries take form, there is beginning to be supporting research and technical assistance for doing it right. In bio-based product development — when it is environmentally sustainable and returns revenues to farm communities where the risks are taken — small companies have potential to be the leaders in doing it right, precisely because the more sustainable approaches are decentralized and customized within the local ecology.

Farms are diversifying to stay in business, sprouting bed and breakfasts, hayrides and cultural programs, museums, craft shops, greenhouses, biodiesel processors and windmills. There is a growth in new business models such as community-supported agriculture, in which customers buy shares upfront to finance the farm's planting and growing season. While political and scientific battles rage as to what constitutes "appropriate" farm technologies, farmers are getting sophisticated with computer applications, from mapping to marketing, and also with organic and biodynamic methods of soil enrichment. Choosing a career as difficult as farming, and then choosing a way to farm that reflects your values and holds some promise of survival is an act of bravery and a path of experimentation. But a new generation of farmers is moving up, and some areas have specific apprentice programs to help immigrants and others enter the profession.

"Farming" usually refers to agriculture, but the term is increasingly relevant in the world's waters. With 69 percent of our fish populations in decline and the population growing at 80 million per year, aquaculture could be a "blue revolution" or a disaster. After rapid growth, the industry is leveling off but still provides an estimated 25 percent of the world's fish.[1] This technology is widely touted as a sustainable alternative. But aquaculture has moved into an industrial mode that has brought a variety of ecological ills, including depletion of aquifers, pollution of downstream waters with wastes and antibiotics, risk of spreading disease from non-native species into wild populations and a massive drain of protein in the form of fish meal fed to big carnivorous fish like salmon. At its best, however, aquaculture can be designed for ecological soundness, for example, by using closed-loop systems to recycle wastes, ecologically sound pond maintenance and water-recirculating technologies. Just the same as with land-based farming, there is much work to be done in developing, testing and commercializing sustainable methods, setting standards and building markets. Healthy fish, meat and produce have expanding markets from gourmet restaurants to "farm to school" programs — and the marketing side of sustainable food production is a growth area too.

Commonly cited national companies producing healthy products and exerting leverage on their industries include Newman's Own (with its recent expansion and organic lines), Ben & Jerry's (dairy), Odwalla (juices) and Muir Glen Organics (sauces and juices). You can find out about hundreds of others, and the industry as a whole, by consulting *Natural Foods Merchandiser* and its companion publication, *Natural Foods Investor*. The marketplace for natural and organic foods is a spectacular growth area, with more than a little Wild West atmosphere. You can now choose between a natural food supermarket, including large national chains such as Whole Foods, Wild Oats and Fresh Fields; the natural foods section in your local supermarket; a privately run health food store; and your local co-op. Employees, too, have these choices. And, of course, the range of work being done goes beyond direct customer service and shelf-stocking to include marketing, purchasing, training, finance and management at the store, regional and national levels. Depending on your values and talents, you could end up managing an organic greenhouse supplying a natural food superstore with fresh salad greens or an e-commerce program for a fast-growing retail chain such as Whole Foods. A key element in the marketing of organic produce is certification of croplands, currently involving over 45 agencies in the US. This is a growth area, especially in the need for field inspectors.

One of the most obvious ways to work in the food business, of course, is to get involved with a restaurant. Alice Waters and other famous chefs have made it a priority to create farm-to-table linkages. The same strategy in more down-home style has been a draw for many local restaurants that attract business by featuring fresh-picked local specials.

People in the food business can help not just by what they serve, but whom they serve. Thousands of chefs have participated in Share Our Strength community banquets against hunger, brought together by the Washington-based non-profit of the same name, to finance nearly a billion dollars of anti-hunger philanthropy.

As complex as the politics of food and farming is the politics of agricultural research. But, from federal and state agencies to higher educational institutions to community-based organizations, a lot of people are working to figure out more politically viable, ecologically and economically healthy ways to produce food and other farm products and help consumers make informed choices. Research and teaching in organic farming has begun in schools of agriculture such as Wilson College in Pennsylvania and the University of California at Davis. Agricultural extension agencies at the state and county level vary widely in their interest in alternative food production methods. On the positive end of the spectrum, many state extension agents have been heavily involved in the creation of a regional system of farmers' markets.

Gardening, a beloved activity for many, is a sister industry to farming and employs many thousands in horticulture, marketing and distribution of products and services. But the National Garden Association notes that this market has lately been stagnant. Thirty-six percent of US homes have a flower garden and 22 percent have vegetable gardens, which translates into a substantial market for gardening supplies, seeds, classes and books, as well as gardening and landscaping services. Only 48 percent of households did their own lawn care in 2005, a sign of opportunity for natural and innovative lawn services as well as the usual kind.[2]

Forests and Forest Products

A major response to the need for sustainable forest product standards is the SmartWood certification program for harvesting sustainably managed woodlots. Because forestry is a global industry, the certification was designed to be applicable to imports as well as US products. The program concretely helps participating companies by providing a marketing support system, which has proved especially attractive for small businesses. Fairly quickly, a network of timber companies, processors, wholesalers and end-users has crystallized to endorse, and learn to practice, a more sustainable form of forestry.

In the larger forests of the US, sustainable practice revolves around restoration of forest ecosystems as well as the development of standards and business models for more sustainable practices. Compared to larger-scale, industrial forestry, many of these jobs are less standardized, more varied. There's work for foresters, resource managers, planters, wildlife biologists, loggers, milling and production workers and transportation people. The sustainable forest economy also includes companies, like the furniture maker Ikea, that purchase certified wood on a large scale. There are substantial opportunities for cottage industry using portable sawmills and independent woodshops and for creating specialty markets in salvaged materials, such as cabinets made from barn doors. Industry groups are working to grow these into a sustainable industry that can scale up as the forests are restored.

Increasingly, common employers are small, carefully developed model enterprises like Wild Iris Forest Products, a prototype processing facility in the

US Pacific Northwest. Wild Iris started up in the summer of 1998 as a model of efficient milling and processing, creating high-quality lumber and flooring out of low-grade tanoak sawlogs. Other employers moving ahead with more sustainable forestry techniques include both industry giants and fledgling companies that are finding their identity and market niche through sustainable practices.

And then there is paper. What was once taken for granted is now a subject of intense research and innovation, from recycled content to bleaching and dyeing methods to commercializing alternatives to wood pulp such as kenaf and hemp. Paper recycling technologies continue to develop, creating work for engineers and for innovative niche businesses in general. So do markets, creating marketing opportunities in both private sector companies and governmental programs. More and more, the ecological economics of forestry is revolving around the spectrum of biological products that can be produced by the intact forest and around the management sciences for optimizing yields while preserving long-term health of the forest and surrounding communities.

Waking up to the Opportunity of a Sustainable Built Environment

Of all the environmental technologies in circulation, the huge cluster known as "green building" is one of the hottest. The healthfulness and economics of shelter are dimensions of sustainability that touches everyone's life. US consumers use more resources than any others, including an estimated 20,000 pounds per year per person of virgin forest products, fuel, steel, glass, cement and plastics.[3] Construction and demolition waste is the largest source of landfill volume — and an enormous recycling market is in the process of coming to life. Green building includes minimizing impacts on land through careful building location and natural landscaping; adopting the healthiest possible materials, including reused and recycled ones wherever possible; and minimizing water and energy use. For many greener designers, the aesthetics of green building has been a highly effective calling card for residential, commercial and industrial clients, as well as communities grappling with the broader questions of what healthy development might look like. This trend goes together with building deconstruction, a gentler approach to demolition that recovers the reusable resources in a structure and sends many fewer tons to landfills.

Green building has attracted such attention because major markets are emerging as more and more cities adopt "high-performance" building guidelines. Training, certification, research and industry development leadership are arising from professional societies like the American Institute of Architects and by a powerful industry consortium called the US Green Building Council (USGBC). The annual GreenBuild conference draws thousands, and major real estate developments such as New York City's One Bryant Park are pushing the boundaries of these technologies and practices. Not only has green building broken out of niche status into a fast-growing industry segment, but lucrative and valuable specialties are emerging in the application of high-performance and environmentally advanced building methods in key industries like health-care facilities and schools. World-changing work is being done by architects, civil and mechanical engineers, material and product developers and by builders in both the residential and commercial sectors, at scales from cottage to skyscraper. High-tech trades like the installation of geothermal heat pumps and solar electric systems are growing. So are service industries such as energy auditing and building performance analysis.

Green building and design is one of the most complex, integrative and fast-moving fields of work today. The skills required to do it right are not only technical — they're also interpersonal and creative, because an effective design for a particular natural and social environment can only be achieved by bringing together everyone who has an interest, from the landscape architect to the heating contractor, not to mention the customer. Upfront costs of projects may be a few percent higher than for conventional buildings, which still gives rise to periodic shakeout in the industry, but these costs are easily made up in energy, productivity and health-related savings. A front-running community in green building is Austin, Texas. A push, started in the 1970s, by a group of architects and designers known as the Center for Maximum Potential Building Systems, to educate and inspire builders, architects, materials suppliers and others, has resulted in a greener building stock for the city, a Green Building project with Habitat for Humanity, a Green Buildings directory and a staff position in the city government called Office of Green Buildings. Larry Doxsey, head of the Green Buildings Office, remembers a tragic but educational fire in a green building project for low-income housing. Chatting with the fire marshal as the blaze was being fought, Doxsey asked, "Notice anything different?" "Of course," said the fire marshal, "no toxic fumes."

More and more major institutions are creating the position of environmental coordinator or environmental manager to address the spectrum of concerns about resource stewardship, pollution prevention and environmental justice. Campuses, hospitals and library systems increasingly have environmental affairs expertise — whether in a special position or in the advanced training of an existing staffer such as the physical plant director. The marketing of more sustainable buildings is growing easier as awareness spreads about environmental health and the toxins that permeate traditional building materials.

Behind the greening of the building industry is a new environmental orientation toward materials and manufacturing more generally. The little manufacturing that remains in the US tends to have a comparative advantage when it is environmentally advanced — for example, IceStone, a maker of high-end countertops from recycled plastic bottles, employs 90 people in the former Brooklyn Navy Yard. Recycled newsprint, wood waste and scrap denim are among the materials now used in building trim, structural panels and insulation, a sign of the scope and innovativeness of this industry and the range of niche businesses within it.

Pollution prevention and waste minimization have become mainstream operating principles for companies that see value in recovering raw materials and in reducing the toxic outputs to be contained or cleaned up later. States are passing toxics use reduction laws requiring industries at least to plan for phasing out toxic substances. "Design for the environment" is also becoming mainstream. The notion of "extended product responsibility" means that, not only will Xerox take back your empty copier cartridge; it will take back your run-down copier itself for disassembly and remanufacturing. Many manufacturers will do this with your car. Research universities like the Rochester Institute of Technology employ engineers and scientists to advance these practices further.

Triggered in some cases by regulatory pushes and in other cases by strategic vision, major industrial companies have phased out specific chemicals and have devoted major research and development efforts to putting safer systems in place. In grappling with compound after compound and process after process, many companies have realized that the wisest strategy is to move far upstream and "design for the environment," rigorously identifying non-toxic materials, processes that minimize waste and design for aggressive reuse and/or recycling using a life-cycle analysis. Because some of the largest companies are those with the most resources, and the financial ability to implement changes when they want to, genuine improvements like these often coexist with entrenched problems and controversial practices, leading to complex career dilemmas.

Some impetus for industrial innovation has come from within companies seeking long-range advantage or avoidance of regulatory sticks. Some has resulted from invitations from government to be proactive, through pollution prevention programs that offer career opportunities of their own. For example, Rochester Midland's development of a major line of safer industrial cleaning agents was prompted by outreach from employees at the US Environmental Protection Agency's Region 2 office in New York City. They, in turn, were driven less by regulatory enforcement zeal than by discomfort in sniffing cleaning residues when they came in to work in the morning.

A great deal of the toxic pollution from industry and small business comes from a minority of industries, such as printing and dry cleaning. Targeted government funding of alternatives, and technical assistance to help small businesses adopt them, has begun to result in cleaner practices. Alternatives have even begun to crop up in the form of franchises such as the "cleaner dry cleaner," Zoots. This illustrates the principle that "much of the innovations that displace established industrial practices actually come from outside them, often from the next generation of entrepreneurs," according to Nicholas Ashford of MIT, a specialist in industrial innovation. Investors are increasingly focusing on these upstart business models, as illustrated by the annual CleanTech Venture Fairs in New York and elsewhere. Startup enterprises galore coexist with more established businesses in state and national Environmental Business Associations.

This trend gives rise to some specific jobs in industry, such as that of environmental manager. It also leads many companies to integrate the same skills and responsibilities into their existing line and supervisory workers — in essence, greening many jobs.

The built environment is shaped not only by private sector development practices, but also by the honored and fascinating field of planning. Planners in towns, counties, regional and state government, consulting firms and in economic development agencies translate ideas about human settlements into concrete designs. They can be generalists or specialize in transportation, urban centers, rural land use, economic development and more. At its best, the planning profession aims to mediate tensions between people, social groups and the natural environment by creating an orderly process for determining common values, shared priorities and elegant principles for transcending conflicts. Therefore planners may find themselves caught in some of the most challenging political crossfire to be found. But they also have the opportunity to educate many sectors and communities.

Creating environmentally benign and socially coherent human settlements also involves preserving open space, and one means to this end is the legal device of the land trust. The Land Trust Alliance reports that over 1600 trusts are now protecting an area 16 times the acreage of Yellowstone Park, a doubling of protected lands in the last five years.[4] Administrative, legal, fundraising and educational professionals work with land trusts, as do hands-on managers who must balance ecological health with social benefits such as unobstructed views and recreational access. Urban land trusts may include housing and social services and can be a key community development strategy for preserving affordable housing.

Transportation is another integral aspect of sustainability and an enormous industry in the public and private sectors. Let us not waste any breath moaning about how we're all hooked on our cars. Let us talk instead about the enormous benefits to health and the environment of moderating this habit and the intriguing range of jobs available in public and alternative transportation. For example, the US bicycle industry has lost the manufacturing competition to China, at least for now, but it is still a $5 billion industry distributing over 19 million human-powered vehicles. And while most automakers around the world have embraced higher fuel efficiency standards and prospered, the major companies in the US still lag and suffer as a result. On-demand short-term car rental businesses like Zipcar are growing fast too.

With widespread awareness of global warming and energy security issues, the once-obscure arena of power generation is becoming a hot (though still small) field. Some forward-thinking public utilities have begun to recognize that they have painted themselves into a corner by defining themselves only as energy suppliers and are beginning to seek niches as energy conservers. "Demand-side management," also known as conservation, is about helping consumers of all kinds (residential, industrial, municipal, etc.) make smarter use of energy. This idea had wide currency in the 1970s, resulting in visionary programs in many states. After an era of dismantling or de-funding these initiatives (which can always happen again!), they are on the rise. In more and more regions (California, Texas, New Jersey, Massachusetts, Vermont), both private utilities and governments are placing their bets on the cost-effectiveness of conservation. Advanced eco-efficiency is an opportunity not only for those who produce products and services, but for users including some of the largest corporate energy and materials users. A sign of the times is the early 2007 announcement of a Climate Action Partnership committed to major greenhouse gas emission reductions for major employers including BP, Alcoa, General Electric and Duke Power.

Quality of Life: Being Human While Preserving the Planet

Humans have adorned themselves for millennia and currently pour billions of dollars into personal care products. Consumer health and environmental concerns in recent years have included the petrochemical base of many cosmetics; the dyes, preservatives and other ingredients which slip through labeling requirements as "trade secrets"; animal testing; packaging; biodegradability of products; and, for the many who still care, the images of women that are used in marketing these items. On all counts, innovative options are available for shoppers, employees and entrepreneurs. Many famous pioneering social ventures have been in the realm of personal care products for a simple reason: you can make 'em in your kitchen. The Body Shop International is emblematic of this business, and social ventures in general, for its bold founding vision, stormy adolescence in full view of a critical press and maturation as a more humble but still ambitious organization.

The textile and fashion industries also have enormous environmental impact. For example, cotton constitutes 3 percent of the world's crops, yet uses 26 percent of the world's pesticides by weight. Other environmental and social issues facing the fashion and fiber industries include water use, soil protection, competition for cropland, toxic dyes and worker health and safety, especially for many thousands globally working in marginal conditions in the garment industry.

Out of this mix, an "eco-fashion" sector is emerging, seeking ways of doing business that are smarter and gentler for the earth, consumers, the workforce and the industry itself. The linkage between environmental protection on one hand and worker health and safety on the other makes this industry one of the most visible zones of opportunity for cross-fertilization between the "environmental" and "social" aspects of making a difference.

Environmental issues in the textile industry are interwoven with worker health and safety concerns, which have been a focus of both international campaigns and enforcement by the US Department of Labor's "no sweat" initiatives. Levi Strauss led the industry in devising and implementing a progressive "global sourcing code" for its branches and subcontractors around the world, which lays out concrete standards for all the company's subcontractors and suppliers in the areas of worker health and safety, child labor and environmental practices. Levi's was the first to implement annual environmental health and safety audits of suppliers.

Major industrial players have discovered markets in "eco-fibers," notably Wellman, Inc., whose Eco-Fleece made from recycled plastic bottles addresses multiple environmental problems profitably and with elegance. Wellman even engineered a Master Apprentice Program, an annual showing of high fashions made from 100 percent recycled soda bottles. Designers have included the most famous like Oscar de la Renta, Tommy Hilfiger and Diane Von Furstenberg, as well as innovators who focus primarily in this area. Linda Loudermilk — whose website proclaims "Change is inevitable," creates classic and quirky designs in experimental natural fibers.[5]

Some of the changes in the fashion business are a result of entrepreneurial inventiveness. Others have come about through the efforts of advocates working with industry decision-makers in a concerted manner, such as Businesses for Social Responsibility's Fashion Industry Working Group. According to staffer Deborah Weiner, "Most of the big fashion labels do not do their own production, so there's a sense in the industry that they don't have much environmental impact." They may understand office energy and waste audits, but Weiner and her colleagues had to do some work to gain acceptance for the idea that a major product brand could influence the production process of its chosen suppliers. The groundwork done by Levi's helped. Weiner's own background in the industry helped her to be an effective change agent.

Tourism is a top global industry and a cornerstone of economic development thinking. It moves people around. It creates infrastructure. It brings cultures into contact with each other. It stirs up commerce. For all these reasons, the direction taken by a tourist industry can be a mirror of the society and a catalyst for change.

One of the simplest aspects of healthy tourism is the world of camping. The 3,200 member camps of the American Camping Association are a subset of the world of specialty camps, conference and retreat centers that lift humans out of their ordinary lives and place them closer to nature (whether a little closer or a lot). Camp counseling is the quintessential summer job, and a growing number of colleges now have associate and bachelor's degree programs in camp administration. Camps and visitor centers, like any other facility, can be designed as environmental showplaces. Many are including leading-edge models in national organizations such as the YMCA, as well as one-of-a-kind private facilities like the Mohonk Preserve Visitors Center in New York's Shawangunk Mountains. The magnificent but simple facility boasts passive solar and geothermal heating, locally sourced stones and wood.

Especially in pristine areas with an interest in preservation, a more evolved idea of ecotourism is gaining attention as a basis for sustainable development. Depending on the context, this can mean everything from camping and hiking to cultural tours to guided trips visiting ecological spots of note. At its best, ecotourism can generate jobs for local guides, interpreters, managers and guardians of protected areas; create revenue streams to fund wildlife preserves in developing countries; and generate commerce for local communities.

At the same time, however, ecotourist experiments have brought grave risks. Twenty years ago, almost no tourist lodges existed in Nepal's Annapurna region. Now, dozens of lodges cater to the tourist trade. The demand for wood to heat the lodges and prepare meals has lowered the forest line by several hundred feet. In his study of the trade-offs, *Handle with Care*, Scott Graham adds that "in the Nepalese village of Ghorepani, which sees an average of 18,000 trekkers in nine months, food and lodging costs have soared, creating inflationary prices for the local people. And yet, without the tourist trade, Nepal would be in dire straits."[6]

No matter how environmentally concerned the participants may be, the hotels, resorts, roads, harbors, airports and other chunks of infrastructure that accompany tourism have dramatic physical impact on land, waterways and habitats. For people in the developed world who are considering work in the travel or tourism industries, the guiding question is clearly, How much restraint is enough? But another question is emerging next to this one, How much positive impact can a well-designed tourism project have?

Many ecotourism guides offer thoughts on questions that the traveler can ask to determine how community- and environment-friendly a destination really is. These apply every bit as much for job-seekers in the industry. For example:

- How does a destination contribute to and interact with the local economy? Does it hire local, shop local and pay fairly?
- Do they contribute to or otherwise support environmental organizations, especially those in the host country?
- Does the destination offer honest, in-depth information about the environmental and cultural issues of the place, including the complexities of its own role and impacts? Do they encourage guests to shop local, volunteer and show restraint by not buying products that harm the environment, such as those made from sea turtle shells, reptile skin, bird feathers, fur or ivory?
- How do they show respect for the local culture, people and wildlife?

Tourism, food production — these are major industries, and they are environmental industries. Kevin Doyle, lead author of *The Complete Guide to Environmental Careers for the Twenty-first Century*, adds, "The boundaries have softened greatly between 'environmental' and general careers. There is opportunity everywhere."

CHAPTER 3

Work that Protects and
Restores Our Communities

Many of the fields of work geared toward social well-being are caught in tensions similar to those on the environmental front. There is push-and-pull between public and private provision of services; between responding to crises and devising more preventive approaches; and between containing costs and doing what's needed. As a result, the work opportunities are distributed among the private, public and non-profit sectors in ways that defy logic; there is enormous diversity in work structures and philosophies; nearly every organization believes it is on the side of the angels in reforming its industry; and the work is being continuously reinvented.

Healthcare is an enormous sector that can make copious uses of skills in medical arts, business, technologies, communication, caregiving and advocacy. The *American Health Professions Education Directory* lists 45 separate professions (audiology, dentistry, epidemiology, nursing, etc.), each of which can be practiced in many ways, with many specialties and at many levels of expertise.[1] As the structure of the industry continues to be in flux, the practice of healing arts involves a mix of healing the patient and healing the system. Out of the turmoil, though, has come a wealth of inventive career directions: MDs who have given up on the managed care system and are developing individualized specialty practices; nurses who are exploring the potential of entrepreneurship and intrapreneurship (i.e., innovation within a workplace); paraprofessionals finding or creating their niches; and practitioners of healing arts who often have one foot inside conventional healthcare institutions and the other outside.

More than half of US adults say they've used some "alternative" healthcare methods, whether herbs or shiatsu or hands-on healing. There is growing research support for "complementary" medical approaches — that is, those that can work along with conventional medical options — and the first accredited training programs such as Dr. Andrew Weil's at the University of Arizona's Health Sciences Center, as well as programs at New York Presbyterian Hospital, California Pacific Medical Center, Beth Israel Deaconess Medical Center in Boston, the State University of New York's teaching hospital in Stonybrook, the University of Pittsburgh Medical Center and the Health Alliance of Greater Cincinnatti. In Britain alternative medicine is penetrating the mainstream to the point that 62 percent of practicing acupuncturists are physicians. In the US there is some degree of integration. The National Institutes of Health now operate a Center for Complementary and Alternative Medicine, which researches a vast range of healing modalities and provides a militantly neutral information clearinghouse. A good sample mapping of the territory is the Center's seven categories:

- Diet-nutrition-lifestyle change
- Mind-body intervention
- Bio-electromagnetic applications
- Alternative systems of medical practice
- Manual healing such as therapeutic touch and reiki
- Pharmacological and biological treatments
- Herbal medicine

Among the richest areas of innovation, for physicians and many kinds of paraprofessionals, are the ends of the lifeline, birth and death. Hospice workers may come from the worlds of medicine, social work, clergy, advocacy and many other backgrounds. The many specialist roles connected with childbirth and parental support include preconception and fertility counselors, maternity fitness instructors, midwives, breastfeeding instructors and advocates and infant first aid and safety instructors.

In addition to their direct services, medical practictioners are discovering several other levels on which they can make a difference. As advocates, people in the medical community bring unique credibility to issues of public and environmental health, from the tobacco industry's influence in schools, to the reduction of toxics use. As an industry, healthcare is taking these values to heart with an ambitious international initiative called Health Care Without Harm.[2] In service delivery and building construction, this initiative supports healthcare providers in removing unhealthy materials, from mercury thermometers to vinyl pipes. Beth Israel Medical Center in New York City, a participant, saved $900,000 a year at the start, through product purchasing and disposal changes including reducing, reusing and recycling. Again, using an established and tested framework developed with industry leaders, anyone working in health-care can make an extra measure of difference.

Healthcare institutions are also developing alternatives to animal research and the use of live animals in teaching, spurred in part by the work of Physicians for Responsible Medicine. At a number of medical schools including the University of Florida's, medical student activism has replaced the use of live dogs for surgical training with audiovisual tools oriented toward human anatomy.

Helping People Thrive: From Social Services to Community Development

Mental health and social services help every community to take care of its own, including providing safety nets for children, elders and people needing care or protection, such as victims of violence or witnesses in criminal trials. Child and elder care, hospice care, prevention of suicide and domestic violence, substance abuse prevention and recovery all fall into this category. Service providers are also natural advocates and policymakers.

Psychologists, social workers, counselors, trainers and professionals with many other titles assist people with personal development and healing. They work in private practices, managed-care settings, schools, hospitals, prisons and businesses. There is a nearly infinite range of schools and modalities to consider, with corresponding variation in educational and licensing requirements. Psychiatrists with medical training and PhD psychologists are still sought after, especially when clinical expertise is combined with management skill and other specialties. However, managed-care systems have led to the replacement of many generalist psychologists with clinical social workers who bring less strenuous but still solid training, yet command more modest salaries. Social workers also find niches in corporate employee assistance programs, helping employees with the spectrum of issues that affect performance, from family stress to substance abuse.

The Age Wave cannot help but create new areas of work including service, advocacy and information. Massachusetts counselor Margaret Newhouse, who offers workshops on finding work you love in the second half of life, ob-serves,

> There are, of course, the social service positions in agencies and em-ployee assistance programs, helping aging adults and their children who may be working full-time and need help sorting out the maze of services available. There are social workers focusing on independent living and others focusing on hospice care. But there is also a wealth of opportuni-ties focusing on older adults who are thoroughly active and constitute a major market.

These include consumer advocates, Elderhostels and other lifelong learning programs, tours and retreats, workplace empowerment programs like Boston's Project ABLE, advocacy groups like the Grey Panthers. "To start networking in this area," Newhouse recommends, "visit your local Council on Aging, join the National Association on Aging and visit websites like ThirdAge.com."

Over the generations, psychologists have expanded their perspective from a central focus on the individual's subjective experience to a recognition of the relationship between individual well-being and the social and environmental context. Family, group, social, community, political and eco-psychologies have developed in the 20th century in recognition of this systems view. Within social work, the field of "macro practice" provides a framework for psychologically sound intervention in whole systems, from organizations to towns to political movements. Shirley Jones, Distinguished Professor of Social Welfare at the State University of New York in Albany, defines macro practice as the realm where "social workers work with large systems and focus on social issues" — for example, applying a social systems perspective in roles as diverse as "legislative assistant, planner, manager of an agency or corporate program, community or-ganizer and economic developer." Long an educator of urban social workers, Jones has culminated her own career with the creation of a seven-year US–Africa partnership to support dialogue and collaboration on intercultural so-cial work and community development between the two countries.

Playing a host of roles from clinician to expert witness, psychologists have been engaged with wider issues such as environmental concerns and the dan-gers of the nuclear arms race, as well as school and community violence. The American Psychological Association partnered with MTV to deliver a national special about violence prevention called *Danger Signs* — with training of community-based psychologists to work in-depth with schools and parents to implement the show's recommendations. The work of psychologists on social issues has also contributed a legacy of new methods for group communication and dispute resolution. Principles of family therapy have been finding their way into dialogue processes on charged public issues such as abortion, thanks to the work of many small training centers like Cambridge Family Institute in Massachusetts and major institutions such as the Carter Center. While many psychologists with individual and family-oriented specialties find ways to use their professional skills in community settings, the field of community psychology itself is coming of age.[3]

Another of the interesting opportunities to blend the micro and macro levels of human development is ordained ministry. In this role, you can move from individual and family counseling to organizational development to community projects, while attending to the more conventional roles of education and ceremony — not to mention building maintenance, fundraising, dishwashing and more. Ministers, rabbis and other faith leaders, through councils of churches, can exercise considerable influence on the policies, services and programs of a local government.

Within the world of law enforcement, too, there are moves toward more systemic approaches, including community policing, which brings law enforcement officers into closer communication with communities and lets citizen groups guide their approaches; and restorative justice, which relies less on prison and punishment and more on helping criminals make amends in ways that transform their victims and the situation.

Economic Development

The work of economic development is not only about bringing some economic activity into a community and hanging onto it, but about weaving that activity into a vibrant, coherent economy whose benefits are felt and whose hazards are contained. People do this working for local agencies including planning departments, economic development bureaus and departments of commerce; nongovernmental organizations including unions and community development corporations; for the community relations staffs of larger businesses; for chambers of commerce, private industry councils and other business groups; and for non-profits concerned specifically with sustainability. They may specialize in business attraction and retention, financing, planning and zoning, entrepreneurship, citizen participation processes, environmental management or economic policy. Combining all these kinds of expertise is a challenge, although this is one of the fields where a knowledgeable and gutsy generalist can do enormous good. Michelle Long, Executive Director of Sustainable Connections in Bellingham, Washington, began by forming an alliance of innovative businesses for mutual support and education; she ended up with a vision for economic development that brought her to the table as the community planned its directions.

A popular blend of community psychology and economic development is the movement to teach and support youth entrepreneurship, some of which integrates social and environmental values with vigor. While some programs, such as Junior Achievement, are run in high schools with faculty guidance, many are sprouting their own non-profit agencies or becoming attached to established business incubators. This makes it possible for customized programs to spring up in response to a community's needs and make use of a community's resources. Trainers and program developers may come from business, non-profit management or casework with youth, or simply step forward and gain the skills to meet the need.

Consider the West Philadelphia Enterprise Center, a true community resource proudly housed in the former *American Bandstand* broadcasting station where the historic dance floor is still intact. The center runs hundreds of interested city teens every season through a Boot Camp on entrepreneurship, weaving in an extra social dimension with presentations from socially responsible businesses and non-profits like City Year. With a growing census of established eco-businesses, including the White Dog Café and the Sheraton Rittenhouse Square Hotel, Philadelphia is home to a wave of experimentation to find low-tech sustainable enterprises that can be run by youth and by disadvantaged city residents. Some of the most inventive and promising of these turn out to be the most holistically designed as they mobilize underutilized human capital to create profitable businesses that meet local needs.

As an aspect of economic development, trade is an opportunity to change the conditions under which goods are produced and to organize consumers in support of more equitable approaches. Pueblo to People, a Houston-based mail-order catalog, links up cooperatively owned and managed craft producers in Central America with consumers in the United States. Even on a small scale, ventures like this need management, marketing, finance and "sourcing" or purchasing. With sourcing comes setting standards for social, environmental and quality criteria. These partnerships provide opportunities for business-building that can greatly increase social stability in an area. Targeted mail-order and web-based marketplaces are on the rise.

ForesTrade is a growing international business that trades in high-quality certified organic and sustainably harvested spices, essential oils and coffee. Founders Sylvia Blanchet and Tomas Fricke spend part of their time in their Brattleboro, Vermont, home base and part traveling to production areas in Southeast Asia and Central America. Married when they both worked in sustainable agriculture in Guatemala, the couple never expected to work together. Fricke had a long involvement in sustainable agriculture, ultimately working for the World Wildlife Fund, looking for ways to protect a major parcel of rainforest in Sumatra and the communities living on it. "This wonderful natural resource was being carved up and permanently diminished. There were farmers squatting where the trees had been, clearcutting leaving steep slopes, erosion washing down into the river below. Everyone could see the devastation. Everyone wanted a solution."

The solution Fricke proposed, creating a buffer zone for the cultivation of non-timber cash crops that can be sustainably harvested, is gaining a global following thanks to numerous experiments. ForesTrade now grows cardamom, pepper, vanilla, coffee and other valuable cash crops organically using a network of small farmers, indigenous organizations and local businesses. Blanchet, trained as a social worker, never expected to be running a global business. Her interests had centered on helping people who had experienced violence, addiction or abuse to recover from deep trauma, which led her to study the methods of indigenous healers. But a family business linking Vermont and the rainforests of Asia and Central America seemed to her like a ticket for rich cross-cultural experiences. Blanchet finds that her skills in social work and counseling come into play on a daily basis in managing an international business, both in one-on-one relationships and in understanding the growing business as a human system.

Non-profits as well as universities are bases for economic development research and innovation. At Chicago's Center for Neighborhood Technologies, David Chandler runs a program called Connections that is pioneering "transit-based development" in the city and its suburbs. The program is working with underemployed city dwellers wishing to become entrepreneurs, partnering them with franchise opportunities in lines of business that belong in a human-scale downtown: groceries, cafés, children's stores, hardware, bakeries, wet cleaning (less toxic than dry), reused goods and more. The program's goal is to create synergistic business clusters near transit centers, reducing the automobile reliance of entire communities. Chandler learned his skills through a series of powerful on-the-job training opportunities, starting with a degree in anthropology and a stint as a social worker. He started up and ran a major food bank, then spent 11 years with Francorp, a major franchise development consulting firm.

These experiments embody some sophisticated economic principles, most of which most people don't want to know a lot about. More to the point, they foster community and restore the linkage between the economic and the social levels of experience. Drawing on the Great Barrington experiments, local currencies are alive in over 60 communities in the US and more globally. Ithaca has its famous Hours. Burlington, Vermont, has Bread, with the currency unit called the Slice. The Pacific Northwest has (Puget) Sound Dollars. They're all locally controlled — of course — but Susan Witt serves as a mix of technical consultant, coach and chronicler of these campaigns and of the broader movement for local self-reliance.

Education and Training

Every town has schools. Many have private and alternative schools, charter schools, Waldorf and Montessori schools, homeschoolers. There are adult education and community learning centers, language and literacy programs. There are childcare franchises with educational packages. There's high-school equivalency training and college test prep. And, beyond delivering, administering and marketing the services, there is development of curricula and evaluation of their effectiveness — not to mention education and training for people who do all of the above. Education, by its nature, makes a difference of some kind. Within this vast field, there are enormous variations in philosophies and strategies as well as educational content, not to mention in the health and financial well-being of workplaces.

Environmental education has expanded considerably in the last generation, with some states having mandated programs and many teachers appreciating the power of the subject to engage students. But environmental careers expert Kevin Doyle sounds a cautionary note:

Environmental education is increasing, but it doesn't always translate into more hands-on opportunities for environmental educators. Often conventional teachers find themselves faced with a mandate to integrate environmental offerings into the curriculum and go looking for off-the-shelf resources to help them do that.

Institutions of higher education have begun to realize what riches they are sitting on, in terms of providing incubators and demonstration sites by applying knowledge to produce real-world change. The University of North Carolina's Keenan-Flagler Business School, the Oberlin College Environmental Studies Center and the Penn State Science, Technology and Society Program are among the leaders in meshing curriculum, physical construction and community involvement projects to green both campus and surrounding community. At Penn State, a project representing several academic departments has helped the community to develop "sustainability indicators" against which future projects can be evaluated. At the University of North Carolina, business graduate students learn about the strategic advantages of getting out in front by embracing sustainable economics. At Oberlin College a world-class architectural demonstration project created the Adam Joseph Lewis Environmental Studies Center, a model of green building techniques including photovoltaic cells, passive solar design and a Living Machine system for metabolizing organic waste into nutrients. Several dozen business schools now offer "green" or sustainably oriented MBA programs, as well as programs in non-profit and public sector management and in business with a community development orientation. These are generally developed in close collaboration with businesses and integrate environmental considerations into the ordinary processes of manufacturing, finance and marketing.

Along with education, but distinct, is the field of training. If good education promotes understanding and principled choices, training promotes skill and reliable behavior. Imagine if just about all the facilities managers of airports, hospitals, universities and shopping malls knew how to use non-toxic cleaning materials, paints, varnishes and carpeting. Imagine if all the cab drivers in your hometown had gotten into the habit of never idling their engines between fares. In all these cases, the technologies exist to reduce environmental harm greatly. Helping people to learn specific new behaviors is called training. Both private and non-profit training organizations are helping to promote systematic change in the ways we do business. Environmental practices like the ones above represent training opportunities working with regulatory agencies, non-profits and development corporations. This is one of many examples of a field that also includes cross-cultural communication, diversity, mediation and business ethics.

A century ago, the ways to work for social well-being were extremely numbered: social work, teaching, health care, law and the then-new field of community organizing. Today, the opportunities are limitless.

CHAPTER 4

Catalytic Occupations

Every industry has its impact factor, and so does every occupation. Here are some that show special potential because of their scale, scope and flexibility.

Communication

Information ecology. Cultural environment. Call it what you will. The messages being transmitted on both commercial and noncommercial media are powerfully shaping everybody's sense of the possible. You can put your presence behind your values by means of the media you choose, the audience and scale you choose from local to global and the ideas you voice. A generation ago, environmental reporting was just coming to life; today major newspapers and broadcast media have specialists on these beats — and ordinary reporters need environmental expertise as well. The communications world is embattled, with struggles for ownership of individual businesses, control of technologies and public accountability. As media outlets proliferate, and at the same time concentrate through mergers and acquisitions, it is hard to chart a coherent and principled course. But good people still get good stuff into print, online and onto the airwaves. *Utne* Magazine, a digest of quality independent media, shows the range of accomplishment with its annual awards, recognizing new magazines like *Seed Magazine*, a sophisticated, edgy exploration of science and culture. In spite of the toughness of the industry, independent magazines are proliferating, many with humane values and fresh ideas. Consider *Valley Table*, a regional magazine about the food and farm culture of the Hudson Valley; and *Fast Company*, a watering hole for people in growing businesses who are interested in innovation, communications technologies, progressive social values and building community.

With the growth of socially responsible business and social marketing comes a new thrust in the public relations industry. PR firms may work with clients that have been on the wrong side of public controversies on how to clean up their image and — sometimes, in the process — clean up their act. For instance, the New York firm Ruder-Finn has experimented with the position of "environmental counselor," helping client companies listen to consumer and citizen concerns and figure out how to change in response. One of the simplest and most popular strategies for doing this continues to be cause-related marketing: tying product profits to a popular charitable goal, as Avon does with breast cancer-related fundraising. Local as well as national companies can do this.

Most major public relations firms have some involvement in public interest campaigns, in many cases facilitated by the non-profit Advertising Council. Founded during World War II as a government information outlet, the Council has brought the world Smokey the Bear, McGruff the Anti-Crime Dog and other bread-and-butter public interest images. The Council has worked with the US Environmental Protection Agency, Natural Resources Defense Council and Japan Ad Agency on a major water pollution awareness campaign.

The work of providing and protecting community access to media (for example, cable TV) involves professionals as diverse as attorneys, organizers, community access TV producers and trainers and the technical staffs who build and run the stations.

It's easier than ever to be a freelance communicator, but as competitive as ever to make a complete living at it. On the plus side, advocates like the National Writers Union have helped to challenge norms in the communications industry to the point that freelance journalists can have some expectation of contracts and payments on schedule. Freelance communications is a superb business to be in part-time, with a backup source of income.

The world of communication also includes the book trade, which is one of the most competitive as the major chains consolidate and position themselves to take each other on. After more than a decade of painful shake-out, most communities still have one or more proud, socially oriented independent bookstores — Book People in Austin, Powell's in Oregon.

Libraries

The world of libraries is diverse, and much of it is specialized. A public librarian may be a specialist in urban or community issues, information systems, youth services or another area. Public libraries make a difference just by existing, and some of the most inspiring cases of librarians' activism revolve around keeping their own facilities funded and functional. Libraries on special topics, or for special audiences, are found in government agencies, trade associations, museums, hospitals, prisons, businesses and non-profit organizations.

The American Library Association's (ALA) divisions and conferences offer a hint of the breadth of this field and the specialties that are well established: intellectual property, intellectual freedom and censorship issues, access to libraries, diversity issues, literacy, information technology and service to business. The ALA's 1999 conference in New Orleans featured a spirited workshop on civic librarianship. A respected voice in the politics of governmental information classification and the public's right to know, the Association has been heavily involved in lobbying in support of public access to information and First Amendment rights.

Information Systems

Managing information and communicating it in useful forms will continue to be an important area of work for people in many occupations, and there is a rise in the designation of people in medium-sized to large organizations as chief information officers to keep up with the flow.

Designing and maintaining databases, generating and applying demographic information and using media tools such as simulations and geographic information systems (GIS) are specialties with wide currency. GIS, in particular, can be used to link up the information systems of many users to facilitate sharing, as the San Diego Association of Governments and many others are doing. It can be used to make a city's neighborhood resources and features accessible to citizens. It can facilitate services such as ride-sharing, as the city of Seattle demonstrates. Programmers, system managers, analysts and technicians are all needed, as are people who integrate these skills with others like planning or information science.

Philanthropy

Thousands of philanthropic foundations are in the business of giving away money. Some are private or family run; others are publicly incorporated. Still others are programs of corporations. Although they vary widely in terms of budgets, strategies and individual impacts, collectively foundations are a significant power source in setting the agenda for social activism and policy.

A small foundation may be little more than a board of trustees with day jobs, a bank account, a brochure and an answering machine. But there are thousands of foundations of significant size and means — from community foundations with a few million dollars' endowment up to the giants of Ford and Packard and Rockefeller. Foundations employ program officers, who bring expertise in an issue such as literacy or women's economic development and who interface with projects through the application phase and when they are funded. Research staffs, field evaluators, financial and administrative staff and managers of the foundation's assets are also part of the workings of a major funding enterprise.

Even large foundations are questioning how to be truly effective partners with non-profit organizations in creating fundamental change. Led by the Jessie Smith Noyes Foundation, which used the clout of its stock portfolio to support a grantee's efforts to get the giant Intel to reduce the environmental footprint of a New Mexico plant, activist foundations are increasingly supporting non-profits with technical assistance and direct collaboration. Established funders, and the creators of new foundations, have been engaged in valuable exploration of the ethics and effectiveness of giving, resulting in new movements such as "venture philanthropy" — investing in "social entrepreneurs" who bring vision, track records and business plans into play. Established foundations such as Echoing Green have become platforms for exploring the criteria for useful venture philanthropy, working along with ambitious new foundations such as the one recently created by EBay's founders.

Even with tiny financial resources, the idea of a foundation can spark creativity and engage people in exploring strategy. Boston educational consultant Jamie Coats shows the power of this approach as a way to teach kids how the world works and the role of money. Coats's organization, Kids' Energy, began by giving $24,000 to 2,000 children in a pilot project in the schools of Portland, Maine, with just three rules:

1. The money can only be spent by kids for kids' goals.
2. The money flows through schools, and collaboratively the adults and children have to design a process whereby the funding is connected to educators' goals.
3. Kids have to tell the world about it.

Coats brings extensive experience in building business-community partnerships, first with Business in the Community in his native Britain and then at the

Center for Corporate Community Relationships in Boston. Kids' Energy is built on a vision of partnerships that link up community leaders and children, give resources to children and celebrate what they do — coincidentally riding the wave of educational and communications technologies such as simple Web page design that can be used with great effectiveness by children. Complementing the vision and experience is a particular talent which Coats has learned to recognize in himself and rely on: "I have a particular skill in helping two different sectors or parties take down their defenses and use the resources that used to be devoted to defending themselves to collaborate on something of value to them both."

Advocates

Here is a cluster of professions for highly results-oriented, strategic and very social people. Among the people who are paid to influence others directly, three major categories are political party staff, lobbyists and organizers (who might focus on labor, consumers or other citizen populations). There are advocates on issues and also advocates for individuals such as nursing home residents, hospital patients, victims and witnesses interfacing with a court system. Some of the most compelling advocates for advocacy itself come from the "turnaround generation," young people who recognize that they are inheriting a world with serious work to be done.

The labor movement ("the people who brought you the weekend") is alive and, in a good many places, well. Annual "Union Summer" events — modeled after Freedom Summer in the 1960s — have brought college students into organizing internships across the country. Union organizers build support for union representation and engage in ongoing education and advocacy. An organizer is usually, but not always, a practitioner in a trade who also has skill in communication, administration, consensus building and strategy. Shop stewards, who generally hold full-time industrial or trade jobs and double in this role, act as advocates for workers or workforces when there's trouble. Some union positions are elected, and others are competitively hired. At the state, national and international levels, union research staffs, pension fund investors and other professionals create organizing strategies and service packages to support the workforce, both while it's on the job and after retirement. The investment of union pension funds, one of the largest pools of concentrated capital, is becoming recognized as a force with major potential to affect federal and state policy. The world of union organizing can be somewhat nomadic, but a coherent path can be forged by attaching oneself to an issue or a constituency.

As technical, administrative and professional workforces adapt to the new world of work, professional unions such as the National Writers Union are making a mark. Many professional societies, like the American Association of University Women and National Association of Social Workers, fight hard as advocates for their members on bread-and-butter issues. Professional and trade associations — for example, in mental health, alternative healthcare and natural food — are on the lookout for legislation that stands to influence members' choices of methods and their ability to be compensated for their work; for example, they watchdog controversies over labeling laws designating nutritional supplements as drugs and licensing requirements for alternative health modalities. The larger associations have national staff who provide member services (such as health benefits), publications, research and direct lobbying.

Mediation

The *Wall Street Journal* announced a few years ago that it had figured out why Rome wasn't built in a day: "No facilitators." Beneath the coy headline, though, was a respectful article about teamwork and communication trainings in the building trades. From ordinary confusion and insensitivity among co-workers, to rough waters between collaborating businesses, breaches in labor-management relations and disputes involving many stakeholders, most of us have experienced the paralysis that comes from workplace conflicts. Mediation, negotiation and related skills are gaining wide respect.

Every time a major social issue or policy initiative comes to life, opportunities for mediation come with it, whether it's youth violence or the Americans with Disabilities Act. Fields making major use of mediation include law, business management, public administration, labor relations and community organizing. For example, Peter Shapiro founded a landlord counseling program for the Cambridge, Massachusetts, city government. He has helped mostly small to medium-sized landlords deal with tenant difficulties in ways geared toward reducing the risk of eviction. His tools included structured training on the business of landlording, one-on-one problem-solving assistance and direct mediation. A master's degree in urban planning plus a certificate from the Harvard Program on Negotiation led Shapiro into this role, to which he was able to bring the added credibility of being a landlord himself.

After a few optimistic years as these professions took hold in the 1980s and 1990s, it became common for mediators to accept that they would make their livings substantially through other jobs or in hybrid careers (such as lawyers, clergy or school administrators). Today, however, the field is reasserting its professionalism and value, with a strong offering of business training and negotiating tips to help mediators earn the revenue they deserve.

Law

Most, if not all, public controversies have legal dimensions. As a result, the range of legal specialties that can be practiced from a public interest perspective is vast. Consider homelessness and poverty, community redevelopment, environmental issues, election law, bioethics, immigration, substance abuse and trade issues — for starters. Most lawyers work for the people with most money, and many lawyers are unhappy with their careers. Seventy percent of lawyers responding to a California survey said that, if they had the opportunity to start a new career, they would take it; 73 percent said they would not recommend a legal career to their children. The institutions and networks of public interest law are being sustained for the long haul by lawyers, paralegals and support staff who think these trends are connected and see the necessity to help lawyers expand their horizons in the public interest. This is the spirit behind the move by Ralph Nader's Harvard Law School class to establish Appleseed Centers for public interest law around the US, to address systemic problems and improve local and state policy. "There's a lot happening out there when you start looking," counsels Elissa Lichtenstein of the American Bar Association's Public Services Division, "and once you find out about a few opportunities, it mushrooms."

Ronald Fox's valuable book, *Lawful Pursuit*, surveys the terrain of public interest law, beginning with national organizations whose mission is to litigate in the public interest.[1] These are not numerous, he notes, but they have achieved significant results and are respected in the profession. Because test cases or class action suits filed by major organizations have the power to affect entire demographic groups, there is high impact to working with organizations like the Children's Defense Fund, Native American Legal Defense Fund, Lambda Legal Defense and Education Fund (gay and lesbian rights), National Organization of Women's Legal Defense and Education Fund, NAACP Legal Defense Fund, American Civil Liberties Union and Natural Resources Defense Counsel, to name some of the most prominent. But statewide coalitions and community projects also offer a wide range of opportunities for high-impact legal practice. The smaller the organization, often, the greater the variety of work available to anyone in it. The practice of public interest law can include litigation itself, research, training community advocates and citizens, teaching in a law school, writing and publication, negotiating. Law firms, companies, non-profits with legal departments, specialty clinics in law schools, government agencies and private practice are some of the venues for practicing law in the public interest. With a strong enough focus, you may identify a need and create a practice — or a project — to fill it.

Banking, Finance and Investment

The banking industry has had its share of struggles with both communities and regulators, leading some banks to target funds for innovative efforts in community economic development and environmental innovation, while the majority remains conservative in their practices. Boston's Wainwright Bank, Chicago's Shorebank and Oregon's EcoTrust are banking and community development businesses set up to invest ambitiously.

If sustainable economics is about forging a link between social values and financial returns, then there's an outrageous possibility of real money to be made by supporting, or participating in, enterprises that serve the common good. It's no longer a new idea that plenty of investors want to vote their values with their dollars. This idea has given rise to a generation of socially screened investment portfolios, socially responsible stockbrokers and financial advisors, a vibrant research sector and national organizations such as the Social Investment Forum to promote this arm of the industry. Early innovators, mostly in smaller firms, have done the difficult groundwork needed to make the concept practical by developing solid enough measures of both social and financial performance to give investors competitive returns. In recent years, the sharply rising level of investor interest has prompted Wall Street to take a fresh look at these upstarts.

Parallel to the growth of socially aware investment, there is an embryonic but growing population of venture capitalists, management consultants, technical advisors and others available in the world of institutional investment to guide dealmakers in evaluating social and environmental impacts of business ventures they are financing. Institutional investors with this focus include private, for-profit companies like SJF Ventures, which invests in growth companies in the clean tech and service sectors that create good career tracks including strong entry-level opportunities. There are also "venture philanthropies" set up by successful entrepreneurs and funds created by non-profits such as the Nature Conservancy, to further their missions.

As companies formalize the notion of multiple bottom lines and environmental accountability, there is also a growing need for ecological economists and a rising appreciation of this role (flagged as one of the 25 hottest careers by *Working Woman* magazine as early as 1996). Graduate programs are attracting students, and attention, at the Universities of Maryland, Vermont and New York. Governments at all levels, banks, private companies and non-governmental organizations all employ ecological economists, with entry level salaries around $30,000 and senior compensation above $100,000.

Ethics Officers

Although born of corporate scandals, the business of business ethics has matured and grown more sophisticated and substantive as companies recognize the motivating power of authentic values — and the disarray and risk exposure that comes from disregarding them. Added to the wake-up call of pure expense has been the 1991 US Federal Sentencing Guidelines for Organizations, which impose heavy fines and strict probation conditions mandated for organizations convicted of federal crimes. The Guidelines contained a brilliant incentive to develop meaningful ethics programs. They decreed that fines could be cut, and prosecution avoided, if companies could show that they had created such programs as a good-faith effort to prevent violations. Very quickly, the high-level position of corporate ethics officer came into being in a majority of publicly held corporations. Their professional society, the Ethics Officers Association, now has a membership of over 500 and sponsors conferences, research, education and a certification program. There is a growing body of research that employee retention, morale and productivity are positively affected by a culture that employees regard as "values-based." Increasingly, large companies are moving their program focus from "compliance" to "values."

John Ferraro, Ethics Officer for Orange and Rockland electric utility in New York State, holds a position that has been designed by building on lessons learned in other companies. Ferraro reports not to the CEO but to the chair of an independent audit committee on the board — "an essential feature to give me the autonomy to do my job." Often his job deals with issues as ordinary and yet challenging as employee conflicts of interest and sports gambling on the job. And his path into the position is also growing more common. He was chosen not for any specialization in ethics, but for his strong networks and credibility in the company, gained through his previous job in building design.

If you hold a title like chief ethics officer or vice-president for corporate ethics, your role will likely include helping to build an internal consensus on ethical standards; crafting a code that is understandable and, hopefully, inspiring; running it by lawyers, top executives, union and shareholder representatives and others; training the workforce in the code itself and in expectations about how they will make decisions; providing some kind of low-risk way for employees to report abuses and get help in handling dilemmas; and evaluating the effectiveness of all you have created.

Creative Artists

Among the most powerful catalysts for claiming and living out new visions are the world's visual and performing artists and the wider community of choreographers, stage designers, conductors, gallery owners, curators, art teachers, supply houses and others — professional and amateur — who keep the spark alive. The high profile of struggles with arts funding in recent years may mask the fact that people do make a living creating, marketing, financing, housing and exhibiting, ensuring, publicizing and covering the arts in the news media, as well as providing for the education of artists at every age and skill level. Successful arts complexes are springing up in post-industrial communities, such as GoggleWorks, a full city block of art-related businesses in a former goggle factory in Reading, Pennsylvania. Commercial art, landscape, fashion and industrial design are among the hybrid areas in which dollars can be made and high standards upheld.

The arts can make a difference by their very existence. Psychologist James Hillman speculates that many of society's challenges come because we are cut off from beauty and lose our way as human beings. The arts can also richly enhance other pursuits — from healing sculpture gardens in healthcare facilities to the experiments of artists in designing beautiful wind turbines that will serve as community totems.

PART TWO

THE TEN STEP PROGRAM
for Principled Career Development

STEP

Wake Up

Intelligence is fine,
but what really matters is awareness.

PHIL JACKSON, BASKETBALL COACH[1]

Who Are You, and What Do You Think
Is Going on Around Here?

What do you think — about your own potential and the changes ahead? Do your beliefs affect what you even try to accomplish? Do you believe that adult development is basically a pedestrian affair, or that big leaps are possible? Do you believe you are part of a wider web of life that's interconnected and interdependent? Do you live that way? Do you believe the work that most reflects your values is worthy of decent compensation, clientele and support? Do you believe you can lead and inspire others? Do you believe that the strength of your commitment makes a difference in what you're able to accomplish?

When is the last time you took stock of what you think about the realities of work, money and power?

The ability to self-reflect is essential to long-term change. But it's one of the hardest skills to cultivate and to integrate into a demanding life. A New York architect friend spoke for many people when he said, "Sure, I have time to reflect on my life — sometimes five minutes at a stretch, if I'm alone in a cab." Without this ability, people can try on new behavior patterns, but can't fit them into an integrated sense of self and therefore can't keep them going reliably. In transpersonal psychologies and spiritual traditions, there is nearly universal attention paid to the "observer self" or "witness," the part of one's being that watches and integrates the rest. Cultivating this capability is demanding, in the same way that exercise and nutrition are demanding — and equally essential. In *Voluntary Simplicity*, Duane Elgin makes the point:

> The crucial importance of penetrating behind our continuous stream of thought (as largely unconscious and lightning-fast flows of inner fantasy-dialogue) is stressed by every major consciousness tradition in the world: Buddhist, Taoist, Hindu, Sufi, Zen, etc. Western cultures, however, have fostered the understanding that a state of continual mental distraction is in the natural order of things.[2]
>
> Consequently, by virtue of a largely unconscious social agreement about the nature of our inner thought processes, we live individually and collectively almost totally embedded within our mental constructed reality.

Self-reflection does not mean self-obsession. In my experience, the people who strike the best balance between introspection and action are those who spend most of their time focusing outward and functioning without undue complexity, but "check in with themselves" with some regularity.

People want to go through life in a conscious way. It's more rewarding and you're more successful. Columnist Colman McCarthy points to the rising popularity of monasteries and other religious retreat centers among people of every conceivable background, who come for weekends and longer spells of quiet meditation, walking and reading. McCarthy, who spent some years in a spiritual community himself "to get some traction before lurching into adulthood," has put his ear to the ground to learn more about this phenomenon. He quotes professional golfer Tom Stewart, who checks himself into Gethsemani monastery in Kentucky every fall for a decompression period that is the opposite of a retreat. In Stewart's mind, it's "an advance — because you go forward" more effectively when you stop to get oriented.

Going to a special place for this purpose has the obvious advantage of screening outside stimulation and distraction. But it also segregates the process of reflection from the rest of your life. Many people prefer to identify places and times for quiet that can fit readily into their existing patterns. One useful approach comes from the late Danaan Parry, a former Atomic Energy Commission scientist who founded the Earthstewards Network and for many years ran workshops internationally on spiritual, Earth-centered living. Following the traditions of many Native American nations, Parry recommended identifying your "power spot" in nature, a place "where you can relatively easily tap back into your Aloneness. It's a natural setting that holds for you the qualities of calm, quiet, wild, earthy, grounded, centered. It is for you only." That power spot is close enough for easy access, yet self-contained and far enough away from human settlement to welcome your whole being, not just the civilized parts. A park or rooftop garden, a meadow on the edge of town — any of these will suffice if they ease you out of habitual ways of seeing and into wholeness.

What's important is finding the time to reflect, whatever is going on. This, in turn, requires paying new attention to the balance of life.

- What does it take for you to find "down time" for reflection and renewal?
- What opportunities for self-reflection exist in your everyday life — morning quiet time, for example?
- How could these be expanded or better protected, even in little ways?

Listen. Question. Listen.

One way to ease into awakeness is through listening: to people, to music, to the sounds of the ocean or the city or the ballpark. Listening is not the same as waiting for another person to finish talking so you can have your turn. Listening means opening up to new experience and ways of knowing, without letting your expectations screen them out.

One of the most powerful illustrations of the potential of listening is a highly effective non-profit called the Piedmont Peace Project. This multiracial community organization in rural North Carolina has registered over 15,000 black voters since the mid-1980s and produced a major shift in the voting record of the region's representative in Congress. The project uses teams who make door-to-door visits in low-income neighborhoods, meeting people who are not already jaded by salespeople or pollsters. Without rushing or being required to stick too closely to a script, those teams ask people's opinions about how their tax dollars are being spent and how well their voices have been heard in Congress. Then activists write campaign materials using the language they've heard directly from their neighbors. Not surprisingly, it works.

Imagine listening, really listening, to people you work with and for and to people you hope will help you in your job search or business development. They have visions, too, and responsibilities. They need a few things from you and have much to offer.

Connected to the art of listening is the art of asking questions. Skillful questioning gets you more than answers. It gets you a relationship of creative exploration with another human being. This creates alliances, and alliances are the foundation of the strategy proposed here. Sam Deep and Lyle Sussman promote the art of questioning as a tool for organizational self-defense in their book, *What to Ask When You Don't Know What to Say: 555 Powerful Questions to Use for Getting Your Way at Work* (e.g., "How will we determine whether or not my performance merits a raise?").[3] The questioning spirit and strategies that they propose for *getting* your way, are also helpful in *finding* your way. Questioning is a clear source of wider and clearer options for the questioner, of course. And beyond this, it can help the "question-ee" to focus on an issue and to break out of mental boxes.

Social change consultant Fran Peavey teaches a potent form of strategic questioning — asking questions systematically in order to uncover a higher order of possibilities in a situation. Strategic questions are those that move you beyond obvious information, beyond yes and no and multiple choice. They invite you to imagine new possibilities and explore the ways to remove barriers. "Look for the long-lever question," she advises — that is, the question with the most leverage to get things moving. For instance, "What would it take for this change to be possible?"

- When have you really felt listened to, in your private life and on the job?
- At work, how often do you listen deeply to other people?
- What could you do to promote more attentive, thoughtful communication?
- What are you waiting for?

Wake up to the Story You Tell Yourself and Others

Questioning is a big-time test of awakeness, and a promoter of it. People's answers will only rarely match your assumptions. What comes out of your own mouth may also contain a surprise or two. So the process is a doorway to another valuable awakening: to the story we tell ourselves and the world, about what's happening and what's possible.

- All the jobs are the same.
- Nobody is going to help me if I take an initiative.
- I'm too old to make a career change.

OK, how do you know?

- Recall a time when you've felt stuck. How did you explain the situation?
- Did you make any assumptions that might have limited your sense of possibility?
- Recall a time when you've accomplished something exciting, large or small.
- Have you made any assumptions about that experience that might limit your ability to build on it?

Interpretations of the past and preconceptions of the future have enormous power in shaping what we think is "realistic" in the present. In the limbo of changing values and tectonic shifts in the global economy, it is dangerous to leave to others the work of interpreting reality. Finding our own words to tell the story of what is happening around us, and in our own lives, is a fundamental act of self-defense. This was cultural historian Thomas Berry's point when he wrote:

> It's all a question of story. We are in trouble just now because we do not have a good story. We are in between stories. The old story, the account of how the world came to be and how we fit into it, is no longer effective. Yet we have not learned a new story. Our traditional story of the universe sustained us for a long period of time. It shaped our emotional attitudes, provided us with life purposes and energized action. It consecrated suffering and integrated knowledge. We awoke in the morning and knew where we were. We could answer the questions of our children. We could identify crime, punish transgressors. Everything was taken care of because the story was there. It did not necessarily make people good, nor did it take away the pains and stupidities of life or make for unfailing warmth in human association. It did provide a context in which life could function in a meaningful manner.
>
> To claim our place in this new story, we must each get fully awake to our part in the old, what keeps us attached to it, our potential for contribution and the environments we need to create to help us fulfill that potential.[4]

What's necessary to rebuild economy and society, to live in harmony with the environment and ourselves, is not just one set of choices. It's a process of making choices with greater self-awareness, a process of learning to learn. The leaps we need to make will only be possible when personal growth is rescued from the puritan ethic and returned to the realm of play and liberation. One of the finest models of this is the town square or tribal council, hillside or coffeehouse where people gather to exchange stories, celebrating their own foibles in the healing laughter and curiosity of kindred spirits.

- Start telling stories about your work history. Just do it, whenever the social occasion arises (in small doses, of course, and paying special attention to the interest shown by your listener).
- If you're one who finds more structure useful, then write, talk into a tape recorder, or barter "listening-time" with a friend who might find the same process useful. Try a "career autobiography" — but define the range of "career" for yourself.
- Or pace yourself with mini-stories — vignettes that have special significance as triumphs, defeats, turning points or revealing episodes.
- Celebrate the strength and resourcefulness of the person who lived through all this and is now on the threshold of something exciting.

Wake up to the Interconnectedness of Everything

A blip on the Tokyo Stock Exchange can disrupt home mortgage lending rates in Kansas City. North Americans' dependence on beef contributes to keeping people in the developing world away from land and water they need for subsistence farming. Whether or not butterfly wings whirring in China can really cause storms in the Gulf of Mexico, as the chaos theorists have suggested, every action we take is part of an intricate web of causes and effects among human communities and the natural environment. Systems thinking is the practice of seeing these connections and appreciating their significance. You are a system of thoughts, feelings, information, unconscious imagery, memory and more, all interwoven and interdependent. You are also part of a complex social and ecological system. You have a choice: to view these dimensions as sources of complexity to be avoided, or as resources to be tapped.

The benefits — and risks — of this stance can be seen in a larger-than-life story I'll share here. It's the story of a man with unusual resources and sensitivities — but he could have gone through life without accessing them. "Chocolate Jon," founder of the Endangered Species Chocolate Company, created an ultimately profitable business after a saga that shaped him personally and professionally, a saga that was possible because he was awake to the world around him and allowed himself to be moved.

A young man with a background in triathlons, Jon dreamed of becoming a chef and training in the fine cooking schools of Europe. But he was broke in San Diego, looking for a ticket to anywhere. He heard it was possible to make good money working on tuna boats, so he signed on as a cook.

"Three days into the trip, the garbage was piling up on deck. I asked innocently, 'Where's the dumpster?' My shipmates laughed. 'Take your pick. Port or starboard,' they said. I said, 'You're kidding.' They said, 'Throw it over or we'll throw you over.'"

Over the next weeks, Jon threw some garbage into the ocean, resisted some, got thrown into the ocean some and gave thanks that he was a former triathlete who could handle treading water until he could get the captain's attention. What he couldn't handle was the reality of the enormous fishing nets, more than a mile in diameter, pulling in dolphin, sea turtles, tuna and countless other creatures, all squealing as they were folded into a hydraulic crusher. He vividly remembers the moment his life really shifted:

One day, I looked in and saw this infant dolphin, about two footballs long. Without thinking at all, I jumped into the water and took it into my arms, and it relaxed when I held it close. Then I looked around and realized I had to swim through about a mile of this rabid, thrashing sea life to get to the boundary of the net. They were all struggling to escape; they knew they were going to die. I made it through and turned and released the baby dolphin. Then, in the net I saw another dolphin and imagined that this was its mother. Instinctively, I petted it, stroked it, then lifted it over the net to safety. I bloodied it and bit my tongue and turned to swim back through this mess to the boat. And then I recognized about 30 or 40 dolphins that all saw that this was the way out. I rescued dolphins all day, swimming in my tennis shoes, until I was exhausted.

Miraculously, Jon was able to go AWOL without being missed and to do it several times more. He became adept at cutting the nets without getting caught. The experience was capped the night the crew decided to have shark steaks and commanded Jon to prepare them; inside a huge shark, 3,000 miles from human settlements, Jon was stunned to find a Budweiser beer can.

Jon parted company with the crew in Panama and made his way to Paris and cooking school. He was soon running a successful catering business working with movie production companies. But he was sensitized for life. He became a rabid recycler and would wash dishes for 200 at the end of a 20-hour day rather than using disposables. When his first daughter was born, he found an extra reason to care about the future. At the zoo with her, when she was four, they were both transfixed at the sight of elephants, shackled, swaying back and forth because this was the only movement they could make. In the car, Jon launched into a lengthy speech about endangered species, human dominance, threatened habitats and the rest. Abruptly he realized he was talking to a four-year-old. "Honey, that was a little intense," he apologized. "Did you get any of it?"

"Yes, Daddy," she replied. "But I want to know what you are going to do about it?" The Endangered Species Chocolate Company was his immediate response. The business deals in gourmet Belgian chocolate, wrapped in packages designed by world-class artists to depict rare species and provide education on ways to stop their decline. Today the company is a good rural employer and gives over ten percent of its pre-tax profits to environmental groups in the form of chocolate for resale.

Chocolate Jon is a well-known figure in the local schools, where he talks to teachers and kids about making their lives count — in every imaginable way.

Enlightened self-interest has a lot to do with recognizing opportunities for creative work that are also opportunities to deepen, and benefit from, human connections. This is very different from seeing yourself as a lone, vulnerable contender, competing with droves of others for a limited range of identical spots. When you take interdependence seriously, competition loses its attractiveness, while negotiation and collaboration are revealed as a path of enduring strength.

- Who do you work for (or, if you're out of work, who do you imagine yourself working for)?
- Did you naturally leap to one answer? How many other ways can you answer it?
- Do you work for an organization? A boss? Customers? Shareholders? The people who rely on your paycheck? A social movement? An innovation you dream about? Future generations? All life on Earth? A few cherished people?
- What are your agreements, spoken and unspoken, with each of these groups?
- When there's a conflict among these loyalties, as there's bound to be, how is it resolved?
- Who, and what, might you work for in the next phase?

- What are your images and feelings about the state of the world?
- Do you read the papers or watch the news? When you do, notice how it makes you feel. [This is not as easy as it may sound.]
- When you come upon stories that are especially moving — maybe inspiring, maybe wrenching — get in the habit of talking about them with someone. Ask yourself: If I were fearless and had unlimited resources, what action would this story inspire in me?
- Finally, what can you, as you are, do?

Interconnectedness Exercise

What's it like to think about all these loyalties? Is it a bit overwhelming? Illustrated below is a way to put them into greater perspective. On a piece of paper, start writing brief phrases to describe problems that concern you. They can be personal, community or global, political, economic or ecological. Whatever

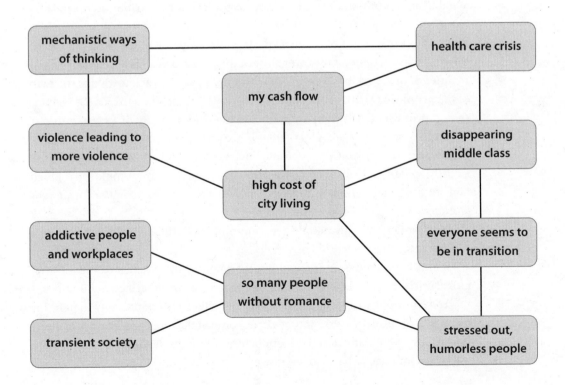

pops up, write it down. Instead of doing it in a list, however, scatter them all over the paper as your imagination dictates. If you have a blackboard or big piece of newsprint, that's even better. When you have run out of ideas, filled up the paper or got impatient to consider what's next, draw lines to indicate any connections you see between problems. They may be cause-and-effect connections. They may have a similar source. They may affect similar people. They may trigger the same responses in you.

According to psychologist Sarah Conn, who designed this exercise:

> Many people have a little "aha!" moment when they do this; they realize that, wherever they choose to take action or make change, the effects will resonate through the web of connection in ways they never dreamed. What's more, taking action in any area connects you to others in a way that opens up new possibilities.[5]

Wake up to the Beauty and Pain of the World

Waking up to our potential and our opportunities for contribution means taking in the vastness of the disarray and danger around us — not in a spirit of blame, guilt or victimhood, but as participants capable of focusing our attention in a way that liberates power. Part of this wake-up call is about the present realities of our working lives. In some ways, it's easier to acknowledge the pain of the people in Darfur or the students of Virginia Tech, than to face the feelings of compromise, frustration and failed actualization many of us carry in our own jobs or job searches. A lot of people are on the edge on the job — an observation borne out not only by seething tensions but by overt workplace violence, a costly epidemic. In an average week in US workplaces, one employee is killed and at least 25 are seriously injured in violent assaults by current or former co-workers.[5]

No wonder so many people get so numb. Unfortunately, this adds up to a self-perpetuating cycle.

James Hillman has an intriguing theory about the essence of the modern global crisis. In his view, it's the fact that people are anesthetized — literally cut off from the ability to resonate to beauty in a vigorous enough way to fight for its preservation. To the extent that's true, some of the most potent lines of questioning for uncovering new work opportunities might be these:

• When and where have I been moved by beauty lately?

- Where can I create beauty? Or preserve it, or make it available more democratically?
- Where can I ease suffering or help to eliminate its root causes?

Joanna Macy offers a lovely meditation to help open your heart to the beauty, pain and connections that make your world distinct. This visualization will assist you in stepping out of "ordinary mind" to focus on how your values may translate into direct engagement with the world. Do this in a quiet, calming setting and give it plenty of time.

Get comfortable, breathe deeply and slowly and empty your mind of thoughts and images.

Now call to mind someone you love deeply. Anyone. Gaze at them, see their face, notice their strength, be aware of how much you want their lives to be free of suffering. Let another image of a loved one arise, and another. Hold them in your caring gaze and feel the particular love you have for them.

Let the circle expand, to include those you see regularly, at work and in the community. See all their differences and quirks and feel the particular quality of love you have for them.

Expand the circle further to include people you see less often, long-distance friends and family, those who are lost but missed.

Include people you have some conflict or difficulty with. From the safe base of this visualization, see them in their full humanity and hold them in a gaze of simple compassion.

Let the circle of empathy widen to include non-human life, all the winged ones, the furry ones, the leafy ones, the single cells. Let into your awareness the wonder of all this life. Hold it in your mind's eye. Feel the particular love you have for all the life forms we share this Earth with.

Now imagine yourself leaping out beyond the Earth and watching this beautiful blue-green orb from a million miles away. See the teeming life, the vibrant communities, the suffering and the stagnant and the happy, healthy ones. See the humans, interacting in a thousand ways with all the other life forms we share this Earth with. Notice where your gaze is most attracted. Stay with it as long as the process is alive. Notice where there is work to be done, to preserve life on this planet and quality of life in human communities. Notice the work that most attracts you.

Finally, when you feel ready, bring your awareness back to Earth, to one of those places you have chosen, and feel the center of your awareness returning to the body you have been given in this lifetime. Come back slowly and when you feel ready, open your eyes.

Take some time to write down your impressions. What aspects of the exercise were most vibrant? Which areas seemed "flat" or hard to visualize? The blanks we draw can be as instructive as the images that arise. How would your "career development" be different if you did it in this state of awareness?[6]

An alternate, more physical wake-up exercise is the Walkabout. Take a walk in your neighborhood or another neighborhood that interests you. Better, meditate and then take a walk. You may want to carry a notebook, but do not lose yourself in it. The idea of this walk is to pull your attention out into the world. Where does your gaze naturally move? What's overlooked? Do you feel drawn to explore a new direction, or to follow a path that's safe and known? What does this reflect about the state of your being?

Simply pay attention to whatever your eye catches. Look at the storefronts, the gardens, the homes with TV lights in their windows, the kids on corners. Look at the downtowns and the malls and the movements of people and commerce. Look at the gardens and the vacant lots and the traffic patterns and the land use. How clear is the air? What vistas are attractive? Where are people thriving? What's growing, and how healthy does it look? What enterprises are at risk? What lives are at risk?

How do you feel about this state of affairs? Does anything make you angry? Sad? Fearful? Bitter? Amused? Excited? Impressed?

Now, step back into thought-mode and speculate. What's the work that led to this state of affairs? (Visualize. Write. Take time. This is juicy.)

What's the work that could make this picture more attractive and hospitable for humans and the web of life?

Seeing, caring and connecting to the planetary drama in all its forms is also a path to seeing ways out of conflict, stepping out of limiting frames of reference and finding unexpected solutions to problems. It is anything but a soft skill. This attentiveness is what keeps life's tasks and projects on track (and worth doing), a fact recognized by more and more enlightened businesspeople such as James Autry, who writes in *Love and Profit*:

Listen.
In every office,
you hear the threads
of love and joy and fear and guilt,
the cries for celebration and reassurance,
and somehow you know that connecting those threads
is what you are supposed to do
and business takes care of itself.[7]

Waking up, above all, means noticing the richness of life around you, seeing how you can enrich it further and realizing how many allies you have in that process.

STEP

Stabilize Your Life

With so much to choose from,
no wonder many of us think we can keep doing a little bit of everything,
and somehow the important stuff will take care of itself.
And small wonder our powers of concentration are so faint
we need written instructions to remember to feed the cat.

— DEBORAH BALDWIN

A lawyer I know cut his stress levels and got in shape at the same time with one simple policy. Whenever anyone wanted to meet with him, he suggested that the meeting be held outside — walking briskly. It worked for him. It didn't do his meeting partners any harm either. But it was a good-sized leap out of the box that most people stay in when considering how they might contain the stresses of life. When you are contemplating a major change, those stresses and sources of gridlock do not make it easier. What gets in the way of seeing your next steps clearly? For most of us, a good bit of it is complexity and conflict in our "personal" lives, which of course touch our working lives in a big way.

One of the strongest reminders of the interconnectedness of the web of life comes when you try to adjust one strand in the web of your own life. Start any-where. Change anything. And watch everything else shift. Switch jobs and watch the changes in your social life that result from the new rhythms of your schedule and your new associations. Start or stop a romance and notice the im-pact on your motivation to job-hunt. Break out of a limiting self-image and watch some of your friendships grow stronger while others fizzle or blow apart because your so-called friends had an investment in seeing you as you were.

At this point, it's fair to say the working public can be divided into two categories: those who have taken some steps to simplify their lives, and those who are somewhere in the process of facing (or denying) the challenge. Some of us are seeing how far we can get by taking baby steps. Others of us are considering how radical we can be, in order to go beyond making our chaos more tolerable — to really create lives of coherence.

We all face different circumstances. But virtually all of us can appreciate two underlying themes. The first is shifting our relationship to time and material needs out of endless cycles of scarcity and excess and into a more steady state, in other words, discovering what "enough" is like. The second is reclaiming a sense of purposefulness in the way we allocate personal resources, including money but also time, goodwill and emotional energy: shifting out of reactive mode and doing whatever we do with deliberateness. Duane Elgin, author of the classic *Voluntary Simplicity*, makes the point that this mode of living isn't just materially simple. It's "voluntary" in the deepest sense — that is, it's about reclaiming control and choice in our lives.

Truly stabilizing your life also includes establishing some kind of right relationship to community and environment. If you live in the Western world, chances are good that you fall into the habit of thinking that you first have to get your "private" self together before you will be capable of being useful "out there" in the world. But if we take seriously the idea of interconnectedness, here's another way the whole picture begins to change. We are highly unlikely to get our lives in balance if they are not integrated into the web of social and ecological community. That's where we get the juice, the beauty, the majesty, the sense of what's important and the limitations to our own importance. Stabilizing your life is not only about balancing your books; it's also about putting them down and heading for a mountainside.

A good tool for reviewing and refining priorities is the Life/Work Wheel. For each category in the following "life/work wheel," make notes about your wishes and hopes for a balanced and satisfying life. Consider the relative investments of time and resources into each category, as they are now and as you'd like them to be. This will be the basis for work in future chapters.

For each category:

• What are some visual images, feelings and words that arise in your mind when you consider this aspect of your life?
• How is this category "working" for you?
• What's strongest about this aspect of your life?

THE LIFE/WORK WHEEL

- What's most shaky about each?
- What would it take to make this area of your life really satisfying?
- In this area, what is one step (however modest) that you could take right away to bring the reality more into line with your own vision?

Considering all the categories and the relationships among them:
- To which of these aspects do you pay the most conscious attention?
- Which of these aspects of your life are most in need of some more attention from you?
- How could you simplify or adapt to make this attention available, at least for a bit, by: (a) letting go of activities? (b) combining or reorganizing activities?
- Looking at the areas that are working best, what strengths or strategies might be transferable to help the others work better?
- How could the elements of the wheel be better integrated in your life?

Stabilizing your life simply means creating the conditions for long-term change in the gentlest, most coherent way possible, reducing urgency levels wherever possible and increasing your resilience. It isn't impossible to be resourceful in the midst of a crisis. But it's easier in the calm zones. Don't worry; we're not going to try to solve all the rest of life's problems before proceeding on the work front. We're just going to open up a little space.

You may be in an acute crisis. Maybe you've just lost your job. If so, breathe deeply and make a plan for the next week, the next month, the next year. Stabilization for you will be financial and emotional and will include helping your family and friends cope with the changes ahead. Two pieces of good news: helping you in this kind of acute transition is what the free support systems of our state departments of labor do best, and while your loss may be great, you just found something that others will envy: time.

Or, you may be in some kind of acute trouble that keeps you pinned in an undesirable work situation (or keeps you from finding work). You may be stuck in a violent relationship, an addiction, psychological struggles or even a job situation so dangerous or demeaning that it leaves very little left of you with which to create a future. If this is the case, please do all you can to break free, starting now. Let the attractive force of more interesting work and a saner life give you the courage to draw new boundaries. Consult the resource list at the end of this book for a lifeline or two.

However, if you're in "just" the usual disarray experienced by a person whose work situation is uncertain, read on. The work of stabilizing your life covers a number of categories:

Surveying the terrain — looking at what's working and what needs attention, what personal and material resources you have and what's missing, which struggles are inevitable and which ones are the result of bad planning; stay awake! while doing this.

Plugging major leaks in the structure — stemming any uncontrolled flows of time, money or attention which keep you from effectively making the changes you want to see.

Removing toxic influences — looking at current relationships (on the job, social or intimate) that may be holding you back and at scars from past experiences that may have unconsciously limited your sense of possibility.

Strengthening the foundation — reinforcing your life-support system in every sense, from education to financial self-sufficiency to the availability of tools you need to make your chosen changes.

This is obviously too much to attempt quickly. But it is a process to begin now and continue with a gentle, steady approach, as if you were untangling a knot of necklaces that have been lying in the dresser drawer for years. That calls for three qualities: finely focused attention to detail; the ability to look at a situation from many different angles and to see the parts within the whole; and high levels of frustration tolerance — which can be cultivated through a mindfulness practice, which is why Step 1 of this program is Step 1.

Along with mindfulness comes taking care of yourself. From Department of Labor offices to church basements, wherever job search support groups gather, you can see the signs of stress and bad self-care: the gaggles of smokers outside, the coffee and donuts. Don't go there. A life transition is a time to take exquisite care of yourself and learn low-budget ways to do that. Here is a starter list for you to build on:

- Take out new kinds of musical records and tapes at the library
- Walk in new neighborhoods
- Go to the museum on free days
- Trade massages with a friend
- Stretch and exercise regularly
- Go for a hike or a boat ride

- Hang out with people of many generations
- Call friends on the phone and pay attention to how they're doing
- Dance around your living room
- Take bubble baths
- Notice sunsets
- Spend time in the natural environment
- Keep a journal
- Read things you don't normally read and get plenty of fiction and poetry in your literary diet
- Draw or make up stories with kids
- Sketch, paint or make collages
- Introduce yourself to neighbors
- Look for free concerts, lectures and performances
- Plant trees and edible flora, or do local environmental restoration projects, with people you want to spend more time with
- Get interesting cookbooks from the library and make new treats
- Sing
- Meditate

This book is being written in a time of economic turbulence, with huge differences in the employment opportunities from place to place. The instability many of us are experiencing (the "lucky ones") is a result of too many opportunities, flawed though they all seem to be. However, we all know in our bones that this situation is not likely to be permanent. Economic cycles, downsizings, globalization and other destabilizing forces make it necessary to face how much of the conditions surrounding our working lives will always be outside our control. Social and environmental innovators must think about recession-proofing and disaster-proofing their working lives, by building kinds of security that do not easily vaporize (such as durable goods, strong relationships and the skill of self-nurturance on relatively little money).

Take it one step at a time. Each step you take toward balance and resilience will make future movement easier. If you are living within the normal chaos range for a working person in an industrial economy, consider what you could do with a three- to six-month Stabilization Plan, starting now. That's not a long time, especially if you are seeing increments of progress every week. This worksheet can be copied and used for each month of the "program" you develop.

Life-Stabilization Worksheet

Aspect of life	Desired results this month	Action steps	Done?
Material Where are the toxic dumps? Borrowed items to return? Broken or missing equipment? Unmaintained systems?			
Workplace If you're working, how can you put your house in order? Got sick time for job hunting? Need to activate contacts? How are your references?			
Relationships Do you have time and emotional energy for friends? Are there important relationships that need attention? Do your loved ones understand and support your present changes?			
Finance What are your basic expenses? What can you do to generate short-term income? To cut costs? To renegotiate debt? To replace financial transactions with neighborly exchanges?			
Balance with the Earth How earth-friendly is your lifestyle? How much commuting does that dream job require? Is a "paperless office" an oxymoron or a possibility? Been outside lately?			
Health and stress levels Are you clenched? What kinds of food are you putting into your body? Getting enough exercise? Meditation?			

Financial budgeting is often the first kind that people do, and it can be a source of the disciplined thought that gives rise to budgeting skills that also work with time and other resources you have. Maine farmer Amy Dacyczyn, publisher of *The Tightwad Gazette*, reminds us of the power of frugality:

> A tightwad tends to be fearless in an uncertain economy. He knows that as long as there is enough money for basic needs, he can live quite happily without luxuries. He knows that there will always be Christmas because he can create it from nothing. He knows he can wring more miles from his old car. He knows he can feed his family well from his extensive repertoire of hamburger recipes. Most importantly, he doesn't feel like a victim of economic circumstances beyond his control. While he might dip into savings for a period of time, his lifestyle need not change. He is in control.

As important as budgeting financially, though, is a time budget. As precisely as possible, estimate the way you spend your time in a typical week. Consider: employment, formal study, personal development, health, rest and sleep, time in the natural environment, social relationships, play, creativity, citizenship, volunteer activities, business ventures. Where might you be pouring energy that isn't high-quality or high-priority? What are your priorities for more attention (or more thoughtful use of available time)? What is one action you can take to stabilize your life by using these blocks of time more creatively?

Stabilizing your life starts with defusing crises that handicap you. That frees you to create an environment which encourages asking the most interesting possible questions and following the answers where they lead. The creation of that supportive environment is inseparable from the quest for nourishing work.

Look and you may find an inventive little way to claim time for you. Margaret Lobenstine, a Massachusetts career counselor specializing in supporting "the renaissance soul," says:

> My husband and I fell in love with each other in '61 and got married in 1965. Most of the time we have been each other's best support in holding on to our perspectives about work and life. At this point in our lives we both have work that often occurs on weekends, so we reserve one weekday every week as our "California days," days on which we do nothing practical, just the way we would if we were away on vacation in Califor-

nia! This gets us out in nature together, listening to music together, sharing journaling notes from separate workshops or whatever we feel like! I highly recommend it!

The best path for reducing dependency on stuff and creating a condition of financial balance might actually be the opposite of the austere self-discipline that some people imagine. Success can also come from a more relaxed, organic approach. Ruth Tamaroff and Michael O'Hara illustrate this in their life as an entrepreneurial couple. Early on, Mike says, they "worked like dogs to be able to get lucky" — he in corporate management and she in a successful small service business. By midlife they had enough of a financial cushion to buy time for reflection, though not enough to stop working permanently. As Michael tells it:

We put our stuff in storage, rented the house and left the country for most of five years. We roamed the world looking for adventure and then for meaningful work to do. We initially went to the Middle East — Turkey, Cypress, Syria, Jordan, Israel, Egypt and India. There we visited Auroville, an intentional community of 1,700 people from 30 countries organized around a central philosophy — to change the world by their own transformation. It is a complicated, interesting place. We got into a chat with a Spanish lady running a quilt factory. Ruth started to design quilts. I started consulting. We stayed for two months rather than two days as we had planned. That was the beginning of our discovery of the joys of plugging in and being useful. It was appreciated. We didn't have to have a diploma or credentials, we just had to have skills and help. When you are an active participant you get all sorts of things for free and give all sorts of things. This was the prevailing ethic there and it became our ethic.

We had been living in a little townhouse in Alexandria, VA. We were battling with the zoning authorities to build a garage to store our stuff. Then we received an audiotape from friends, of Joe Dominguez' revolutionary training program, "Your Money or Your Life." We retreated at a friend's country cottage to get immersed in this over a weekend and sort of slapped our foreheads and said, "We're building a garage to put stuff in — why not have less stuff?" We called the architect and said, "Stop!"

The combination of low-stuff and flexible expectations allowed the couple to travel the world, sharing their business skills and learning volumes about how indigenous communities produced wealth while preserving their environments. In Bali, they lived in a village that had cultivated rice for thousands of years without depleting the soil and lived self-sufficiently while leaving time for delights like a gamelan orchestra.

When it was homecoming time, they settled in the small city of Hudson, New York, where Ruth's skills helped her move into fair trade marketing of crafts; Michael found his way into a role as Commissioner of Public Works for the city. A world of lessons about sustainable design of settlements came into play as he took on the role of helping a small riverfront city redesign its infrastructure to conserve water and energy. As this book was going to press, O'Hara had left his public works role and was running for mayor. As a volunteer with control over his time and a global network, he brought substantial strength to a city in need of coherent new leadership strategies.

If you are a wild and restless sort, you may be tempted to ignore this chapter and keep thriving on chaos. If that works for you and doesn't drive your loved ones and co-workers mad, fine. But please note that bringing more balance into your life does not mean giving up on all adventure and risk. It just means choosing risks more consciously.

Create a Vibrant Support System

Build community.
It will help you out a whole lot more than money
when things start to fall apart.

FRAN PEAVEY, AUTHOR AND ACTIVIST

In Cartersville, Georgia, there is a halfway house for southern Baptist ministers who have been fired, mostly for opposing racism within their congregations. When it was opened in the early 1990s, the political balance in the church was so delicate and the passions were so high that people of the cloth were being sacked at the rate of one per week in Georgia alone. The house is named for Thomas Holmes, an Atlanta pastor in the early 1960s who welcomed the first black parishioner into his church — a Nigerian exchange student — over the protest of his all-white congregation. Modest but welcoming, Holmes House provides a haven for others who have taken similar risks.

From barn raisings to business incubators to local exchange trading systems, the homegrown principle of voluntary, neighbor-to-neighbor assistance is being rediscovered on a large scale. Everywhere you look, people are figuring out new forms of community. Some of this help is strictly material. But some is on a different plane. It's about mobilizing the power of multiple minds and imaginations to help individuals move through transitions, make decisions and sustain action.

Co-ops, clusters and collaboratives are coming to life in all sectors, with a diversity and vitality that suggests this idea is permeating the world's cultures. It's more and more common for cooperation to be seen as a source of business strength. Consider what happened in Los Angeles when Charlie Woo from Hong Kong set about invigorating a rundown section of the city by creating an Asian-style business cluster rivaling New York's garment district and the farmers' markets of many cities. With ten adjacent buildings and a distribution company in the family, Woo reached out through Asian networks to attract complementary businesses including a number of competitors. His gamble created a Toytown that generates more than $1 billion annually and employs 4,000 people.

Not only in business is there a resurgence of cooperative inventiveness. One of the more innovative consumer models is the Eco-Loan co-op, pioneered in Santa Fe, New Mexico. It's a revolving loan fund financed by affordable investments by member households. One at a time, households invest in energy- and water-saving improvements from low-flush toilets to solar collectors. As these devices pay off in terms of resource savings, members repay the co-op, and the funds are available for the next borrower. All this happens, of course, with a healthy measure of sociability, show-and-tell and shared wrestling with the dilemmas of lifestyle change.

Do you "cocoon," to use Faith Popcorn's term for hiding out in the coziest possible domestic nest every moment you can? When you socialize, do you seek out a diverse crowd or stick with people who think and dress and play the ways you do? If you tend to isolate, or to hang out with people who don't challenge you, why?

Consciously creating a support system helps you navigate through a desired process of change because it brings you several indispensable ingredients:

- Structure — a backup to your internal "enforcement" system, for making sure you follow through with the actions on your plate
- Focus — pulling you out of yourself and drawing your attention to the significance of your actions in the bigger picture
- Psychological unsticking — suggesting new ways to view old dilemmas, reminding you of your strengths and resources
- Normalizing of experience — taking those secret frailties you think are uniquely yours and showing you, often with a chuckle, just how ordinary they may be
- Concrete resources — suits, software, childcare, shiatsu, with the convenience and personalized touch of barter
- Access to new social and vocational networks, which are gold

Some highly effective support systems are:

- Newsletters, blogs, zines and websites uniting people with common interests and/or common values
- Personal coaches who provide practical and moral support within a framework of personal resourcefulness and responsibility
- Success Teams and similar structures, including Career Change Groups using this very book
- Mentoring, which is enjoying a major renaissance in the business world, with fewer rules and more room for inventiveness than ever
- Incubators, i.e., a location devoted to startup projects, offering shared resources such as phones, work stations and computers and sometimes subsidized overhead. May also incorporate training, technical assistance and mentoring systems.

But there are also many meaningful support systems that aren't created only for that purpose. Consider your ethnic tribe, community-supported farm, bridge club, basketball team, faculty meeting, union, chat room, social gang, salon, board of directors, mentor, business association, hiking club, choir, singles network, coach (athletic or personal — same idea), house of worship, café, child care cooperative, business incubator, book club, tango class.

In 1979 Barbara Sher published a gem of a career book, *Wishcraft*.[1] In contrast with the common focus on individual introspection, personal effort, private struggle and edging out the competition, Sher talks about cooperation. Reflecting an emerging understanding of the social aspects of career development and personal growth, she raises the heretical notion that we do not have to spend our lives working out the past before we can create a vibrant present and future. She shows that, by consciously creating and utilizing a social support system — relying minimally on professionals and primarily on peers who voluntarily exchange services — you can reengineer your life in keeping with your values, passions and talents. Sher has taught thousands how to create "Success Teams," one of the many models taking root today as people grapple with the combination of self-reliance and peer support that they need to flourish. This notion has, of course, been picked up and adapted by many; at this point, it is simply "in the air." It breathes new life into the process of creating our livelihoods by shifting the responsibility onto each of us for creating our lives and attracting the resources we need.

Cliff Hakim describes the necessary attitude shift well in his book, *We Are All Self-Employed*.[2] It's about independence: taking initiative, taking responsibility, making your own meanings out of what's going on. It's also about interdependence: looking for synergies, attracting support by giving support and so on. The attitude that's dangerously obsolete, in his view, is one-way dependence.

Ever say to yourself, "I have to solve this by myself. Otherwise it won't be meaningful"? Human beings may be too adaptable for our own good in many respects, and a prime example is our ability to function for extended periods as though we were encased in Plexiglas. Consider a new ethic: support equals accountability. In the words of peace educator Tova Green, "Support means getting so close to someone that the only way they can move is forward."

Something powerful happens when people see themselves as part of a healthy, functional community and have a positive experience of that. They learn to value themselves because they feel valued. They learn to trust because they're trusted and because others come through. They are able to see their struggles and complaints as part of a pattern, shared by others and with causes that the community can address much more effectively than the individual.

Emotional isolation is a great equalizer, affecting people at the top of an organization as much as everyone else. As a (revealingly) anonymous former CEO wrote after sinking into depression and losing his job,

> Executives and managers, especially those high on the organizational chart, are particularly vulnerable to depression; higher equates with lonelier. Self-protection dictates one can't unburden one's emotional weakness with subordinates or competitive peers — or anyone else for that matter. The ultimate in emotional isolation is the chief executive. He can display no weakness, admit to no doubt or fear, and few, if any, subordinates would dare broach the subject of his mental well-being with him.

Many readers of this book fall into another prime category of people who are at a special risk for being in isolating situations at work — those who are in flux in terms of values and may be changing in ways that are frightening to co-workers and managers. The more you struggle with "outsider" feelings, the more attention you need to pay to building a community where you feel at home.

Some of the highest-powered support occurs when a group is part of a social movement — a large subculture of active citizens working to accomplish a desired set of changes that stand to have a wider impact than their private self-interests. When you are part of a living movement, and a fellow participant comes to you for help — with networking or employment or investment or whatever — you want to come through, not only because you care about the individual, but because the work itself is critical and you both recognize that. Many value-driven enterprises have made a discovery similar to Sylvia Blanchet's when she began to recruit employees for ForesTrade in the United States:

> We would get 70 or 80 résumés for an ordinary job in our little town in Vermont. We got applications from people across the country, with PhDs in international trade, from multilingual Indonesians, from people making six-figure salaries who hated their jobs. Way above and beyond what we are doing directly, our business is succeeding because so many different people want it to.

People who share your civic, creative or entrepreneurial passions can be fabulous supporters if your life experience has given you some. If not, the well to drink from is what the social science researchers call your "values subculture" — that is, that community of human beings who see the world more or less like you do and want to see some of the same outcomes you do. This does NOT mean ghettoizing yourself among people who think alike in every way. It just means making sure you are in regular contact with a core group of people who share enough of a common vision that you don't need to explain the basics, and who see it in their enlightened self-interest to help you out. True kindred spirits are not the only support system you'll ever need. They just give you a very strong foundation for creating the others.

Along the way to clarifying what's essential about the path you hope to follow, it becomes possible to brainstorm about who your "community of concern" really is. This is another way of asking, Who do I really work for and who else wants to see the same changes that I do? When you have a good working definition of this community (or communities), then you can get more concrete by identifying the organizations, social networks and other specific avenues of entry. These are connections to cultivate or deepen.

With this base, it becomes much easier to accomplish the other kind of community-building that is necessary to make a fulfilling career transition and to sustain the work ahead. This, of course, involves building webs of relationship that include the people you don't have so much in common with. Research on the use of social networks to facilitate career change indicates that it is most useful when there are several "degrees of separation" within a network. In other words, it gets interesting when you go beyond surrounding yourself with friends who understand and nurture you, and you then use the strength of that network to reach out to their friends and colleagues and on through several layers. This brings you into contact with people at new levels of influence, in new communities and with fresh worldviews.

When you have some clarity about "who," the next question is "how," that is, how to transform a bunch of static relationships into active, reciprocal, resourceful support. As a reminder of what *not* to do, consider the definition of networking offered by one female executive in *Members of the Club*, Dawn-Marie Driscoll and Carol Goldberg's study of high-powered corporate women: "hanging out with people you don't like."[3] Varying this theme, here is a reminder from Jeff Reid about what can happen when networking is not done in a spirit of community:

> You can always use a friend. Unfortunately, some people take this idea a bit too literally.... Friendship — a traditional value if there ever was one — has increasingly been eroded by that scourge of the go-go era: networking.
>
> Networking, of course, derives from the ancient Anglo-Saxon words *netw* and *orking*, which translate to mean "not working." Indeed, the old meaning still rings true: Today's networker most often covets a gig...
>
> Who among us, in our search for meaningful human contact and meaningless fun, hasn't been detoured by those craving only business contacts? There are few things more annoying than thinking you've found a new pal, when you've really just found another amiable hustler on the make, calculating a career move.[4]

This brings us to the difference between utilitarian networking and community-building. The former rises and falls with your needs; the latter is sustained and sustaining. If you are part of a healthy community, it will come through for you when you need to network. In fact, the shared values of your community will greatly contribute to transforming networking from a chore into a pleasure. The best networking occurs not when you are merely looking for a job, but when you are looking for a way to accomplish work that matters to you and your contacts as well.

Leslie Bender is a painter and decorative artist who is self-employed and therefore constantly on the lookout for projects. She exhibits and sells her own paintings and also does decorative murals, faux finishes, portraits and other projects for clients. Dare Thompson is an arts administrator who confesses she "can't draw beyond third grade level." She just returned to the Hudson Valley community after several years out of state and was looking for an interesting community arts organization to run. They found each other in a career development group and — completely by intuition — began a committed peer supportive relationship that quickly bore multiple fruits. They attended event after event as a team, introducing each other to everyone they knew and thus opening doors to their complementary networks. They co-hosted parties and exchanged all sorts of day-to-day favors. Within a few months, Dare was hired as Executive Director of the Hudson Valley Writers' Guild, and Leslie's plate was filled with projects. Moreover, they had made the entire process big fun.

We are all inventing our own forms here. There are very few firm rules about how to make use of support from your community. There are just a few principles worth noting, based on frequently asked questions and frequently made mistakes:

1. Set about getting what you really need by structuring the process for manageability — for example, breaking down a tall order into a series of modest requests from different people.
2. Make time for the process itself and the people you meet through it.
3. Give back richly when you receive help.
4. Take stock of the process frequently so you can change course as needed; don't expect it to work without adaptation.
5. Be clear with yourself and with others about what you're asking for.

Some people prefer to address their support needs intuitively. But there is no harm in orchestrating it more overtly, as long as you are giving back in kind and operating in a spirit of community. Hide Enomoto, who left the Japanese system of lifelong employment to do advanced studies in Organizational Development and Transformation at the California Institute of Integral Studies, then returned to Japan with a vision of planting seeds of a work ethic geared toward "right livelihood" there. Starting out with a Rolodex and a desire to be more conscious in giving and receiving support, he began classifying people according to the kinds of interaction he tended to have with each: emotional depth, playfulness, analytical conversations, concrete assistance and so on. That part was fun. Then, in his own mind, as he said:

> I deliberately created different kinds of support groups for different categories. Of course some people are suited for multiple needs. By categorizing people according to their real strengths, I have learned to get the best support of the kind I need at a given time. Even though this sounds like "reductionistic" thinking, it has proved to work for me.

One of the best ways to target a healthy support system is to make it an overt criterion in the workplaces you seek out. Carolyn Shaffer and Kristin Anundsen's *Creating Community Anywhere* reports a number of important experiments in redesigning workplaces in this spirit. For example, at the Quaker Oats plant in Topeka, Kansas, workers having problems of any kind that affect their job performance can receive peer counseling from co-workers. Initiatives like this have so much power to transform work, and at the same time so much potential for dangerous backfire, that they are a rich topic for discussion in researching any potential employer.

In exploring the potential for community in a particular workplace, the juicy discussion comes when you've gotten below the generalities. ("Oh, yes, we have lunchtime speakers and volleyball and we all love it here.") The authors of *Creating Community Anywhere* point to eight qualities of vibrant workplace community that have been identified in research. The presence or absence of each of these can be investigated by the resourceful job-seeker. They are:

1. Alignment of values (among workers at all levels and the organization as a whole)
2. Employee-based structure, reflected in ownership or open-ended responsibility
3. Teamwork whenever possible
4. Open communication (for example, face-to-face dealing, two-way performance reviews, open financial books)
5. Mutual support
6. Respect for individuality, reflected in diversity of people and flexibility of policies
7. Permeable boundaries — for example, between union and management

roles, between work and social life and between the organization and the outside world

8. Group renewal.

Certainly, finding a workplace that reflects those principles is one of the premier strategies for keeping your overall support system healthy. If that's not the reality for you right now, look for the handful of kindred spirits on the job. Even one makes a difference. For example:

- A group of seven Harvard employees meets monthly for coffee and brainstorming help toward their shared goal of becoming former Harvard employees.
- Two women, who are employed by different branches of the same workaholic non-profit organization, stay in touch by phone for support in their shared goal of maintaining balance in their lives and refusing work that goes beyond their negotiated schedule.

To me, the move toward reinventing community and making use of social support is one of the most encouraging social trends out there. And once we give ourselves permission and pay attention to what's possible, it's amazing how natural these processes are. It may be a jungle out there. But jungles are home to much more than predators. They are webs of interconnection and interdependence of the highest order. Humans, too, are capable of integrating collaboration and competition in ways that are life-affirming.

I first witnessed the power of a support system in the hardest class of my college years, Physical Chemistry. Known as "the bone-crusher course" for chemistry majors, it required a tough problem set each Monday morning. After struggling in isolation with the homework for many weeks, I took myself for a walk one frustrating Sunday night and saw a light on in the Chemistry building. This was a surprise, since the building was theoretically open only on weekdays. In the library, 85 percent of my classmates were assembled around tables. Several who had part-time jobs in the lab had opened the building with their keys. Pizza crusts and a guitar were strewn around, and a dog slept in the corner. The group was hard at work on the homework — collaboratively. Each table of students had taken on a cluster of problems.

This gathering was a weekly ritual, I learned. It had arisen almost spontaneously in the first weeks of the semester. By dawn the problems would be done and the answers would be shared. Everyone in the room would have a decent understanding of where those answers came from. Those who found the subject easy stayed awake until dawn with those who were having a harder time. That's the part that has remained in my memory all these years. Rebelling against the rules, this group of students did not fall into an exploitive mentality, but a collaborative one. True, these secret sessions played hell with the grading. But they unblocked us all enough that we were able to learn something.

The Kitchen Cabinet

From native tribal councils to corporations, groups of nearly every description have used the ceremonial council as a place to ripen ideas, examine scenarios, engage in serious deliberations and give voice to commitments in the presence of witnesses. But few individuals have realized how well this model can be applied in their own career development. I have experimented successfully with a slightly formalized version of the "kitchen cabinet" for clients in transition, and I encourage you to adapt this idea to suit your needs.

The basic ingredients are these:

1. A "brain trust" of reliable friends and colleagues, chosen for varied expertise, diverse perspectives and having their own lives well enough together to be credible as sources of wisdom.
2. A conference table, which could well be a dining room table, with refreshments, note pads and enough space for resource materials.
3. A facilitator, who basically moves the agenda along, makes sure everyone is heard, feeds back major discoveries and helps dissolve confusion — taking responsibility for process, but not for the outcome.
4. A note-taker or high-quality tape recorder, if desired.
5. An open but on-purpose attitude.
6. A focusing question or questions you'd like the group to help you with and the background information that's needed for them to put the situation in context. This can be written and shared in advance, or spoken in the opening section of the group, with time for clarifying questions before the group launches into problem-solving mode.

I know I want to use my communication and design skills, but how? Why have I been unemployed so long?

→

It is outrageous that so many of us have lost the ability to give and receive help, exuberantly and with pride. This is a skill that is eminently worth relearning. The more exuberant, irreverent, resourceful and focused we can be in giving and receiving support with people who share our values and goals for changing a bit of the world, the more we will be able to weave together a fabric of meaningful work that will make a difference.

What can I do differently?
How will I research the viability of my idea to open a nutrition counseling center and natural foods restaurant?
What do I really need to know?

The brain trust can clarify what's been happening and what may be missing; share from their knowledge about the fields you're interested in; spot limiting assumptions or blind spots in your presentation; point out avenues of opportunity that haven't occurred to you. They can also, if desired, serve as an ongoing support system. In several cases, groups of half a dozen or so have divided up the role of "phone buddy" for the friend-in-need, each making a call or two during a designated week to check progress and offer encouragement. The first time I tried this, it was with a friend who had been abruptly fired from a job as director of communications for a small non-profit organization. A seasoned writer and editor, she was sabotaging herself by sending out résumés full of typos, putting on an optimistic face in public and spending her days watching television. By the end of her evening "kitchen cabinet," her friends had sent her back to the computer until the résumé was flawless. Then they each thought up a few networking contacts and divvied up the support calls to keep her on track in the weeks that followed. She was reemployed, in a better situation, before the six weeks of her scheduled support had run out.

It may seem like a stretch to ask people to devote a few hours to helping you think clearly about your future, but consider how much more effective this is than the hours they would otherwise spend hearing you whine. When you extend the invitation, have a clear description of the process and your expectations. Give them an opportunity to bow out gracefully, so that the group you convene is wholeheartedly present.

EXERCISE: Identifying and Activating Your Support System
(as it stands right now — revisit this frequently)

1. Your core personal and professional support system
   Who can you call for emergency help, moral support and truly honest feedback?

2. Your key mentors
   Who in your orbit is wise, has high credibility and expertise, is clear thinking and takes an interest in your career?

3. Your "access network" into specific sectors
   What doors would you like to see open in the next six months to a year?
   Who do you know who can help you build the bridges?
   How can you get their attention, and how can you help them out in return?

4. The bigger support system:
   Who will benefit if you succeed in your work?
   Who else is engaged in similar efforts or working to create a climate where your work will flourish? How would you describe the "community of concern" that you fit in on the basis of your values and the issues that move you?

5. Support-building activities
   Finally, where are the events and projects where you can further your vision and at the same time meet more people who can become part of your support system on all these levels?

STEP 4

Understand the Landscape

*If we knew what we were doing,
we wouldn't be calling it research, now would we?*

ALBERT EINSTEIN

In learning the landscape of opportunity, there are four important stages:

1. Scoping: what's out there?
2. Investigating: what are the various industries, occupations and opportunities really like?
3. Prospecting: where are the specific opportunities of interest to you?
4. Evaluating: how does a particular opportunity measure up to your criteria?

This may sound obvious, but it is really useful to evaluate each stage separately and make sure you are "done" before letting it go. The stages may overlap, but for example, make sure you have done broad enough scoping to know the range of opportunities before zeroing in on some. Especially if you suffer from a shifting sense of focus, it's important to map out the range of options and be as explicit as possible about the reasons when you do choose among them. As Fred Friedman, a research librarian for the US Environmental Protection Agency, observed, "The key step in getting a grip on almost any research process is framing your questions in ordinary, simple English that is meaningful to you."

In the age of information overload, scoping can be refreshingly easy — at least to begin. This is true, thanks to two big benefactors: the government and Google. The major motherlode of government data, accessed via the US Department of Labor's *Occupational Outlook Handbook* (labor.gov), identifies, defines and describes every occupation that the Feds have managed to take note of. Included are industries with positive and negative job growth and links to state websites for more localized information.

The next step I recommend in scoping out fields is simple, in theory — a Google search on "jobs in" with your occupation or industry of interest. Now, of course, it is up to you to sort through the tens of thousands of entries and find the few that are concrete, thorough, current and credible. Let's take each of these considerations in turn:

- *Concrete* information has supporting data and examples, citations of sources. It has definitions of terms. It has detail. It may even have points and counterpoints to show the complexity of the picture.
- *Thorough* information has a clear scope and fills it in, in a detailed fashion; it takes time to move through, but you gain a real picture of the field of endeavor where you may be spending some years. It's hard to describe but easy to recognize.
- *Current* information, on career fields, is often limited by the time taken to collect data; beware of an article just published, but with data that is three years old! How current can industry and workplace data be? Double check anything more than a year old!
- *Credible* information is from a trusted source — trusted to be honest and knowledgeable. This doesn't necessarily mean an unbiased source. For example, trade associations publish a great deal of career information on behalf of their industries, and may generally paint a positive picture, but their credibility rests on the identification of downsides and challenges.

If you identify a manageable handful of online resources that meet these criteria, you should be able to get a decent picture of any industry and occupation — in general.

The next step is to refine that picture for your area and level of experience, understanding the subtleties of the industry, its growth, controversies and challenges, and where the work is. The best way to do this is by finding *one* really good source of information — for example, a staff person in a trade or professional society, union or interest network revolving around that industry. One of the common errors of informational interviewing is to pick a source who is friendly, or accessible or successful in their position — all good things — and expect them to have an overview of the field, which they may or may not have. The *Occupational Outlook Handbook* refers you to associations, as does

The Encyclopedia of Associations, available in many libraries. A second excellent source is a reference librarian. Another is a career specialist in a school that trains people for the industry in question. These kinds of experts have two things in common that make them very valuable points of entry for your research: they have concentrated knowledge, and they are paid to be available to help you. Make use of this. You can learn as much in a focused hour of interviewing as you can in weeks of hit-and-miss networking lunches.

Three key questions not to forget:
• Where are the good jobs advertised in this industry?
• Where do people go to network and learn about this industry?
• What do people read to keep up on contracts, grants, project developments and other news in the industry?

After you have investigated a given industry on a factual basis, it is time to get a more subtle, human feel for the work, the culture and what it takes to be successful. This is the time to talk with more individuals — and especially with successful ones.

If you like what you are seeing and are ready to move into specific job prospecting, there are two dimensions to the quest: building a thorough picture of the publicly available job listings and gaining access to the invisible ones, the so-called hidden job market. Here's what to do:
• Collect and review *all* the publications where jobs in your field of interest are advertised — including small newsletters, which are often where small- to- medium employers start.
• Develop the best possible prospect list of all the potential employers in your geography that meet your criteria and systematically check their websites for job postings. Use Yellow Pages, association member lists and online databases.
• Review key trade publications for info on new business in the industry and, wherever a contract or grant is reported, sniff to see who is being hired to implement it.

In sorting through information in each of these stages, realize that very little of it is free of bias — overt or intrinsic. "Bias" does not mean willful distortion, but simply a point of view or other selection criterion that determines what questions are asked and who is asked. Most of the time, when people collect information, it is for a purpose — either commercial, public interest or personal. And so, even when intentions are pure, there is a bias. You can counter bias by considering the probable viewpoint of each source and by consulting multiple sources and by stepping back to ask at intervals, What have I really learned here, and how solid are my facts? Fact-check any information you rely on as a foundation for your career choices.

Has Company X reduced its toxic emissions by means of a thorough pollution prevention campaign? Or has Company X reduced its reported data on the US EPA's *Toxics Release Inventory* by moving a couple of factories to Poland? Did Non-profit Q just have a major shakeup because it's mounting a visionary new initiative and the old staff couldn't stand the heat, or because its CEO was worse than useless and everyone finally jumped ship? Or are there other factors going on that you may not have considered?

Excesses of "shallow green" marketing and greenwashing have flown back in the faces of many companies, creating a climate of somewhat greater conscientiousness in communication than existed a decade ago. But it is still important to have one's antennae out for green marketing hype. Bill Walker's rant at a 1991 marketing conference is every bit as true now:

> Green garbage bags. Green gasoline. Computers, hamburgers, compact discs; all here, all green, already. In California, where I live, supermarket chains that refuse to stop selling pesticide-dusted grapes are trying to promote themselves as environmentally correct because their pickle jars are reusable (you know, you can stick flowers in them). They're getting away with it. An oil company is forced by federal regulations to put a few bucks into preserving wildlife habitat, so it spends 10 times that much to buy newspaper ads patting itself on the back for obeying the law. Do people buy it? People do.[5]

If that credulity is a handicap for consumers, it is many times worse for the job seeker. Overcoming it requires literacy on the issues, as well as skill in asking questions and integrating the answers. This skill can only be cultivated through lots of conversations: with employees of a company you're considering and with people, representing a range of views, who have reason to pay attention to the company's practices (for example, union representatives, community activists, colleagues in professional and trade associations, local government and Better Business Bureau people).

Every workplace has its strengths and limitations, contradictions and trade-offs. The same company can be doing great with workplace safety in Bangalore and lousy in Nairobi. Or it can be ahead of the curve in some areas but not others. For example, some of the most technically advanced, serious environmental management systems are in use in the tobacco industry. Especially when you are focusing on aspects of an employer's performance that might be controversial — from employment practices to environmental laws — here are a few questions to ask frequently when evaluating information:

- Is there a precise definition for terms being used? A "progressive" workplace is in the eye of the beholder. "Natural," "earth friendly" and "green" are in the eyes of the beholder, whereas "Certified organic" is based on a precise definition mandated by state (and, one of these days, federal) law.
- If an achievement is being touted by an organization, is that achievement required by law or by the settlement of a legal claim, as many waste-cleanup and pollution-reduction measures are? Does it amount to compliance with regulations, or is it an out-front initiative?
- Is the issue being brought to your attention a priority topic, or did you just let your local chemical company distract you from its toxic emissions by sponsoring a TV special on the rainforest?
- If an employer expresses commitment to a social or environmental principle, how is that commitment reflected in formal programs and budgeting?

There are many useful approaches to questioning. You may want to write down specific questions, or more general lines of questioning; you may think in advance about your goal and then wing it on the details. Whatever style works for you, listen thoroughly and digest the answers consciously. Where's the information? What are the assumptions underneath? Who says it's true? How recently? What did they have to gain or lose?

One of the most enjoyable things to be good at is asking questions. While this skill comes naturally to some of us, it can be cultivated through listening and practice. Here's a truly wicked way to develop your critical questioning skills. It's an exercise called "Talking Back to Telemarketers." I'm embarrassed to admit that I have actually done this. When Brad from Opinion Dynamics Corporation calls you at dinner time, sounding like he's reading from a script designed by highly paid psychologists, instead of hanging up or answering the questions with businesslike numbness, pretend that Brad is a long-lost friend and is actually interested in meaningful dialogue. Take your time in answering the questions. Add juicy tidbits. When you're given multiple choices, consider options that aren't on the menu. Toss some questions back and ask Brad how he feels about them. Probe the assumptions underlying other questions. Give the poor guy some usable answers, but make him work for them. The game here is twofold: to face down a totally scripted conversation and get comfortable setting your own agenda and to become aware of your "hot buttons" that may be pushed in your mind when you are confronting confusing or distorted information. Give the poor guy some information eventually, but get some value out of the conversation yourself.

Beyond identifying sources and questioning skill, it is valuable to think through an overall strategy for drawing out information without exhausting yourself or your sources. How you make use of the information resources out there is partly a matter of style and skill. Some people actually enjoy making cold calls but break into a sweat at the thought of going to the library. For others, it's the reverse. Still, there are inherent strengths and limitations to every information source. For example, consider these differences between hard-copy sources (print and on-line) and direct human interaction.

Hard-copy sources offer a wider scope, but may give you fewer of the subtle signals that are available in face-to-face conversation.

Hard-copy sources are updated at intervals, which may or may not be known. Human sources are updated continuously. That is, people keep learning (some more than others).

You can use hard-copy sources for hours and hours, and nobody gets tired except you. The most valuable human sources tend to be the busiest people.

Therefore do as much information gathering as you can by consulting non-human sources. Then look for people paid to help, such as reference librarians, including those at specialty libraries who can often be wellsprings of info. Use meetings with people when they have the most distinctive benefit — generally when you have done some tentative scoping and want to verify and refine your impressions, move into exploration of fields and then network for specific opportunities. You need people most at the beginning, to get an overview and recommendations on resources and, in the final stages of research, to answer questions that you haven't been able to address and to test out your conclusions. Other useful guidelines are to:

• Focus on questions that the interviewee is uniquely qualified to answer and that will make a major difference in the decision you are facing (for example, be very careful of expecting individuals to generalize on "what it's like to work in this industry" based on their own experience).

- Offer information in return when you can (from your research using publicly available sources, being very careful not to breach any confidential conversations).
- Plan lines of questioning ahead; if that's difficult, second best is stating your ultimate goal or quandary and asking, What do you know that could help me with this decision?
- Take no longer than half an hour, unless the conversation is taking off like wildfire and your source begs you to stay.

In prospecting for opportunities, keep in mind the vastness of the "hidden job market." Only a small number of jobs make it into general interest publications like newspapers. To track opportunities in a given field, consider the factors behind the creation of a job: a market, a regulation, a grant or contract. Look for these, and the jobs will pop up.

For example, many emerging job fields, from pollution prevention to transportation planning, tend to ebb and flow with changes in government regulation and incentives. And so, going upstream to follow the changes in policy will tell you the direction of the emerging work opportunities. That same upstream strategy also means tracking the flow of foundation funding, and private sector investment, in order to know where the work is about to occur. This requires an understanding of the field, which takes some time. But it's more empowering and typically generates more leads than waiting for the actual jobs to materialize. The trick is to identify a small number of key information sources to monitor for your specific interest, including trade publications, association newsletters, databases on grants and major publications such as the *Wall Street Journal*, the *International Tribune* and the *Chronicle of Philanthropy*.

As you identify opportunities, here are More than Twenty Questions to help in evaluating them.

About Each Particular Job

1. What's the fit between the job description and your goals/hopes?
2. What's the pace? Are people around you considered hyper? Is it typical to work nights and/or weekends?

3. How will your performance be evaluated?

4. How about the attractiveness and comfort of physical setting? (Consider lights, noise, cleanliness, smoke, organization of workstation or office and your freedom to adapt it to your needs, occupational/environmental hazards including potential for injury from computers and other equipment.)

5. Will you have access to tools you need?

6. What's your budget and support system?

7. Where does this position stand on the organizational chart (and what can you determine about the informal power available to you)?

8. Why did the last person in the position leave it?

About the Work Environment

1. How much mobility is available — up and/or around the organization? Does the culture encourage lateral moves? What training and development opportunities are there to help you expand responsibility if you want to? Are there multiple career tracks with increased recognition (e.g., scientific/ technical, managerial)? Do educational benefits such as tuition reimbursement apply to all employees, or just selected classifications?

2. How are decisions typically made by your potential colleagues and supervisors?

3. What's the culture like?

4. How much flexibility is there in scheduling? (Consider formal programs such as flextime, job-sharing, telecommuting and family care leaves of absence. Consider also the informal attitudes toward them: How much are they used? Are the patterns of use fairly democratic? Are they associated with lack of ambition or commitment?)

5. What is the ratio of salaries allowed in the organization — from the highest-paid executive to the lowest-paid go-fer? Are there formal guidelines to promote pay equity?

6. Is there an Employee Assistance Program or similar source of support for people with personal problems?

7. Is there support for childcare and other kinds of dependent care? How does the degree of support compare with other employers of similar size in the same field?

8. Are there programs for quality management, skill sharing, teambuilding, etc.? Are they loved, hated, ignored or some of each?

9. Are there opportunities for community service with co-workers, whether it's a little bit on a regular basis or a sabbaticals program for long-time employees?

10. What's the organization's record on occupational health and safety? This is important not only in factory situations but for professionals who use many kinds of lab or office technology. Consult regional offices of the federal Occupational Safety and Health Administration and the Coalitions on Occupational Safety and Health which exist in many states.

About the Workplace's Social Performance

1. What's the mission? What does this enterprise aim to do in the world?

2. Who are the stakeholders affected by the success of the enterprise? How is each stakeholder affected (ideally and in actual practice)?

3. How have decisions been made about physical siting of the offices, plants, etc.? Before the organization was here, what was here? What's the story behind their departure?

4. What specific programs does the organization have to contribute to the well-being of the surrounding community, financially or with service? What kinds of reviews do they get in the communities affected?

5. What local and federal taxes has the organization paid in the last few years? How does this compare to revenues?

6. Does this organization publish a social audit (as, for example, member companies of the Social Venture Network do)?

7. Would you give the product or service of this organization to someone you love as a gift?

About Environmental Performance

1. Are endangered species or resources affected by the company's practices?

2. What is the organization's record on resource use and waste handling? If it's a manufacturing company, does it tend to rely more on pollution prevention or control?

3. How are products packaged? What efforts have been made to minimize solid waste, use recycled packaging materials, etc? Is there an office recycling program in effect, and is it taken seriously?

4. How are environmental policies different in the organization's US and foreign operations?

5. Are products or processes tested on animals? If so, are alternatives being developed?

6. What efforts has the organization made to improve its environmental performance? For example:
    • Have performance goals been set?
    • Does the organization subscribe to formal environmental management systems such as ISO 14000 or 14001 and/or to a code of conduct such as the CERES Principles?
    • Are there incentive systems for environmental excellence for individual workers (e.g. awards, bonuses)? How about for the organization?
    • Is there a commitment to regular eco-auditing, with public reporting of the results?

Of course, there is one more information source for understanding those behind-the-scenes dimensions of your potential workplace: the job interview itself. Conventional wisdom suggests that we are never supposed to have a candid conversation in an interview — and in fact it is a formalized ritual (to be discussed more in Step 8). But do not rule it out, especially where the workplace is one for which you have high hopes. For the purposes of this discussion, there are two kinds of work situations: those where you think you're a good fit in terms of values and really want to bring your whole being to work; and those where that isn't the case, but for some reason you want to be there. Situations of the second kind obviously require circumspection. But situations of the first kind invite a more expansive approach. Advance research will help you to set your trust meter accordingly.

When you make a conscious decision to bring these additional levels of dialogue into an interview, here are some guidelines for preparing and helping to set the agenda:

1. First, establish good rapport and let the interviewers' agendas get taken care of.

2. Use open-ended questions to draw others out and get information that's relatively free of the bias of your expectations.

3. When raising a difficult question, try hard to show how your concerns are compatible with the enterprise's mission and can contribute positively to the organization's success.

4. Draw on your knowledge of industry standards and best practices.

5. If you open up a discussion topic, be prepared to follow it up in a way that shows your knowledge and mature judgment. Be prepared for success as well as barriers. For example, what if the interviewer says, "So, how would you go about reducing the carbon emissions in this plant?"
6. Continually test the waters and have a safe change of subject ready.

Information is only power if you can deal with it. When you begin to consider all you'd like to know about the work opportunities out there, it is easy to get crazy. But, if you want to make choices you can live with long term, you must become a synthesizer and interpreter of information, in order to stand clear of other people's assumptions and value judgments.

Becoming an information warrior, willing and able to track down data and wrestle the meanings out of it, is also wonderfully empowering. It's a step toward being subject rather than object in life. You may experience the distinctive sense of creativity and personal power known to reporters, researchers, private investigators and others who make sense of complicated stories. You rapidly learn that there is no formula to follow — you have to trust your intuition and judgment, and so you do.

In the process, you recognize how big a difference there is between data and information. Data is piles of unprocessed facts and assertions. Information is data interpreted and organized according to some kind of meaning. Meaning is what you draw out and what you have to rely on in deciding your direction — not just in choosing the next step, but in moving effectively along the path from there.

Potential Employer Datasheet

Name of organization _____

Address _____

Phone/fax/email _____

Position(s) of interest _____

Contact person, address, phone and title_____

_____

_____

What does the organization do? (What's the mission? And what are the methods for accomplishing that mission?) _____

_____

_____

Form of organization (e.g., non-profit, family business, government agency) _____

Number of employees _____

How big is the organization's impact?

• sales volume (if business) _____

• budget (if government agency or non-profit) _____

• number of clients served_____

Who owns the organization? (If a business, who are shareholders? If non-profit, who is on the board of directors?)_____

_____

Stock trends (if business) and other indications of health _____

_____

Significant historic events (e.g. changes in products/services/reorganizations and strategic plans/controversies) _____

_____

_____

Potential Employer Evaluation Sheet

Use this form to list positive aspects of a potential job (+), aspects about which you're
neutral or need more information (?) and drawbacks (–).

1. Job satisfaction factors

+	?	–

2. Work environment factors

+	?	–

3. Social performance factors

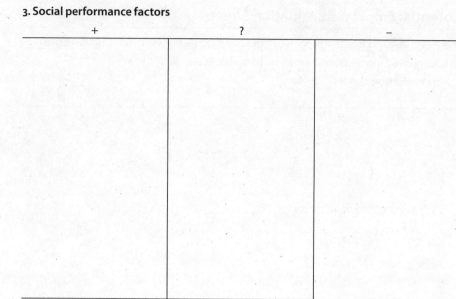

+	?	−

4. Environmental performance factors

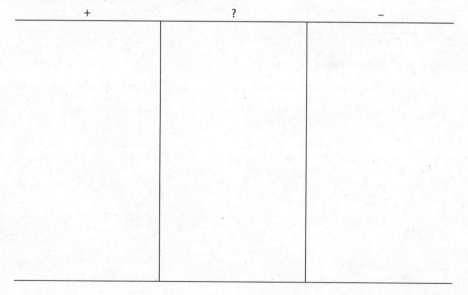

+	?	−

STEP

5

Understand Yourself

S elf-employment, in the highest sense, means finding or creating work that stretches you as well as satisfies you and yields maximum benefits and minimum harm in the world. This step is about the "you" part of the picture: what moves you, attracts you, concerns you, inspires you in your world. Specifically, we'll work with three dimensions:

- What you're good at
- What you like
- What you value and where you want to have an impact

Each of the exercises in this section will take a modest block of time, half an hour to two hours for most people. I recommend structuring those times in and working with this material steadily over a few weeks. Obviously, go where the attractive force is highest, but give each exercise a try. At the end, be sure to devote enough time and attention to evaluating what you've generated and how the elements fit together. This step contains a good deal of work. Do what you can. Use what you learn. And stay with it. As Joseph Campbell once said to a student who complained about the workload in his course, "You have your whole life to finish it, you know."

Aptitudes and Skills

I'm biased. I believe that what you care about is more important than what you're good at. If you are guided by attraction and commitment to something you value highly, you can learn enough of what you need to know. Still, what you're good at, and what you're most comfortable doing, is a factor in deciding among multiple paths of action.

Aptitudes are natural tendencies, as opposed to cultivated skills. In most areas, formal testing services can be found for establishing with high statistical reliability what your aptitudes are. Alternatively, the test of play and experimentation can work quite well.

The skills you have to market and apply are the ones expressed in your work history and the rest of your life. The standard way to get a handle on them is to list accomplishments, both those that were honored by external rewards and others you personally value. Pay attention to the verbs.

Accomplishments Worksheet

For brainstorming purposes, list here as many accomplishments as you can think of, in your work history — or since your last résumé update. If you are blessed with many, first list major categories and then subdivide them for more detail. Use verbs that clearly show the skills that you bring to the table.

1 _____

_____

2 _____

_____

3 _____

_____

4 _____

_____

5 _____

_____

6 _____

_____

7 _____

_____

8 _____

_____

9 _____

_____

Go through these accomplishments and refine your statements to be clear on the impact factor. What impact did your actions have on all the bottom lines you care about, from profits and market share to acres of forest saved and infant mortality reduced?

Once you have this exercise done, you can pull together the skills you've used, both specialized and general. For each cluster of skills, highlight the strongest accomplishments to show that skill at its highest level.

Besides specialized skills of one trade or another — and often more critical for open-ended transitions — are the transferable skills that keep you functioning and effective in any situation. Once they were called "soft skills." We know better now. A very basic laundry list of overall skills and strengths for a successful career is the US Department of Labor's SCANS, outlined in the left column below. You can do a simple self-evaluation, or ask a friend or colleague who knows your work to offer feedback:

Skill	When have you exercised this most effectively?	How would you rate yourself on this skill?
effective participation		
leadership		
interpersonal relations		
negotiation		
teamwork		
self-esteem		
goal-setting and motivation		
career development		
creative thinking		
problem-solving		
listening		
oral communication		
learning to learn		

Much more important than specific skills, which are learnable (even the "soft" ones), are the more general functional capabilities that apply to any situation. Business writer Steve Bennett proposes the following list of basic survival qualities for the "ecopreneur" (and applicable to all values-based working people today). These are not aptitudes, exactly; they are choices:

- Ability and willingness to keep highly informed on changing regulations, competitive factors and emerging markets
- "Foresight and pioneering courage" due to the innovative nature of many businesses
- Especially high ethical standards, due to the sensitivity of consumers and cohorts in the field and the public's wariness of "eco-scams" and "eco-marketing campaigns"
- Ability to deal with very knowledgeable, vocal, activist consumers, requiring an unusually high degree of skill in customer service: "Ecopreneurs must go beyond the traditional rules of customer service and view customers as partners who can help them shape better businesses."
- Finally, true ecopreneurs are driven by a special passion — to heal the planet. That commitment often gives them an extra edge when it comes to weathering the psychological and fiscal storms they will inevitably encounter as they grow their fledgling enterprises."

Personality, Interests and Preferences

How much importance you place on the personality you have today depends to a great extent on how much you expect it to evolve, which in turn may depend on how well developed your skills of adaptation are. But it's useful to have enough self-knowledge to avoid raging mismatches. Serious introverts probably shouldn't rush into a sales career. People with a love of bright color should probably avoid the great opportunity in the bland office. The psychological testing industry offers a cornucopia of instruments to shed light on different dimensions of your temperament, interests, aptitudes and the conditions in which you are most at home.

When you are at one of life's Square One points — either starting out or in deep transition — and you want to look beyond the known universe of possibilities, a good organizing tool is a standard test called the Strong (and its variant, the Strong-Campbell) Interest Inventory. This very simple multiple-choice test invites you to reflect on what you've already done and consider how much you enjoy working with your hands, with language, with concepts and so forth.

Most career centers on campuses or in the private sector can administer this test or guide you as to where to go.

For a deeper sense of your journey, there is a wealth of awareness tools and typing systems drawn from depth psychology, including:

- The Enneagram, a nine-point system drawn on Sufi mystical teachings and Western developmental theory, focusing on the psychological agendas we all bring from our experience with trauma and healing.
- Archetypal systems such as the Heroic Myth Indicator developed by Carol Pearson and Sharon Sievert, including such archetypes as the Warrior, Caregiver, Magician and Wise Ruler.
- The seven energy centers or chakras, used as a basis for self-discovery by popular authors including Rick Jarow and Carolyn Myss.[6]

Tools like these can be valuable in holding up a mirror, but can also short-circuit the process of understanding yourself on your own terms. I urge you to be a smart and critical consumer, try a variety of evaluation systems if you try any and reject anything that does not absolutely ring true. As Jarow writes in *Creating the Work You Love*, "It is up to us to find our own voice, to choose from our own place of clarity and power."[7]

Uncovering Your Values: Icebreaker Questions

1. *Your dream job*: What good work do you daydream about — what does it look like in detail?
2. *The job from hell*: What, in your mind (or your experience) is a "job from hell"?
3. What accomplishments are you most truly proud of?
4. What have you fought for in your work and elsewhere in your life?
5. Who are your heroes and role models?
6. What have been the roughest times in your working life? What values were behind your responses and survival strategies?
7. How are you different from when you started to work for a living (assuming that's more than a month ago)? Who are you becoming?
8. Consider people you've been meeting lately, especially those with whom you've clicked. What do they seem to have in common? Do you notice any differences between new people in your life and the more long-standing relationships you keep up? What does this suggest about your emerging values and sensibilities?

9. If you won an all-expense-paid educational experience — from a field trip to a degree program — anywhere on the planet, what would you study and in what ways? What would you be attracted to in that experience?

10. What volunteer activities have meant the most to you in recent years — from service projects to citizen activism, anything you've been involved in? What volunteer activities have looked attractive, but haven't quite drawn you in?

What does each of these answers reveal about your values? What are its implications for the kinds of work in which you'll thrive and contribute?

Naming and Prioritizing Your Values

Consider the values listed below. Add any others that occur to you. Reflecting on your history and checking in with your intuition, which of these values do you consider very important without compromise (VI); fairly important, depending on the situation (FI); and generally less important (LI)?

accountability	holistic ways of thinking
achievement	honesty
advancement opportunities	intellectual challenge
approval & recognition	keeping a low profile
autonomy	leadership opportunities
caution	leaving work at work
contribution to general knowledge	living where I want to live
contribution to organization	meticulousness
contribution to people in need	money
contribution to social change	multiculturalism
cultural opportunities	nonviolence
democratic workplaces	organization's health
diversity	pace and rhythm of work
educational opportunities	physical challenge
emotional expression	power
environmental sustainability	security
excitement	social contacts
flexible policies such as scheduling	spiritual development
helping others	spontaneity
high ethical standards	stature (social/professional)

time for life outside work   variety
vigorous competition
Other values not on that list: _____

_____

_____

Let the list settle and make sure it's complete and accurate. Then consider whether it can be better expressed in some other form: a poem, a collage, a painting, a symbol. Whatever you end up with, post it in a visible place.

Values in Context

You have named some values that are primary for you. Now, how do they translate into practice? Suppose you value "healthy living." Does this mean you want to eat right and get to the gym every other day, or that you want to work in an office built with state-of-the-art nontoxic materials, or that you want to make sure that the projects you manage are nonpolluting throughout their life cycle, or…?

Choose a small cluster of values you consider important to you in your working life. Now explore, by talking or writing, how you want each value to guide your action. As much as possible, consider what that value suggests for your relationships with all the different stakeholders your choices will sooner or later affect. For example, these include:

- You — your overall career development
- Your family and other close relationships
- Your community
- Cultural and ethnic groups you're a part of
- Cultural and ethnic groups you're not a part of
- Co-workers
- Competitors
- Bosses
- Customers
- Investors/funders
- Other species
- The ecology of your bioregion
- The planet as a whole
- Future generations

How might you recognize a workplace where these values are taken seriously?

Values Evolving

Next, the "Lifeline" exercise turns up the light on the direction of your movement through life and what's emerging in your sensibilities about life and work. On the six timelines below, note major phases and changes during your working life. Along each axis, note major themes and milestones. In that inviting blank space after "today," note ways in which you think you're growing and changing. Be aware of how far in the future you're able to visualize.

When you started	Today	Chosen future

Values _____

_____

_____

_____

Skills & strengths _____

_____

_____

_____

Accomplishments _____

_____

_____

_____

Characteristics of a favorable work environment _____

_____

_____

_____

Desired environmental contribution through work _____

_____

_____

_____

Desired social contribution through work _____

_____

_____

_____

In each area, how do you describe your "growing edge"?

A popular related approach is the "spiritual autobiography." It's nothing more than a heartfelt narrative of the way you've moved through life: the work you've been attracted to, the civic work and community projects you've participated in, the vision that animates you. Some questions to guide your writing:

- What's distinctive about the way you have moved through life and the gifts you are most interested in giving?
- What experiences have been most formative?
- What major social and political events have had a lasting impression on you?
- What major events in the natural world caught your attention or influenced your path? What messages have you gotten from the world around you about the work that's needed? That's rewarded? That's off limits?
- How has the particular evolution of your life shaped the vocational quest you're now on?

Making a Life

What we pay attention to is often what we build up, while other areas of life can wither for lack of attention. Working lives encompass everything that feeds our work and everything that is fed by it, from family relationships, to education and training, to the civic action that protects our career options. The Life/Work Wheel is a visual approach to looking at these dimensions in relationship to each other. The separate schematics are offered to address the clusters of related questions below each one (you may want to photocopy the page and then write your notes alongside the various categories.

For each category

1. What are some visual images, feelings and words that arise in your mind when you consider this aspect of your life?
2. How is this category "working" for you?
3. what's strongest about this aspect of your life?
4. What's most shaky about it?
5. What would it take to make this area of your life really satisfying?
6. In this area, what is one step (however modest) that you could take right away to bring the reality more in line with your vision and goals?

THE LIFE/WORK WHEEL

Considering all the categories and the relationship among them:

7. To which of these aspects do you pay the most conscious attention?

8. Which of these aspects of your life are most in need of some more attention from you? How could you simplify or adapt your life in order to make this attention available:

   > *By letting go of activities (at least for now)*
   >
   > *By combining or reorganizing activities*

9. Which areas are working best? What strengths that you exercise in those areas could be transferred into the areas that need attention?

10. How could the elements of the wheel be better integrated into your life?

11. Now, focusing on your plans or hopes for your working life — however specific or general they may be at this point — in what ways can your awareness and choices in each of these areas of your life make a difference in the process of career change?

12. Based on this assessment, how would you sum up the changes you hope to see in your life as a whole and the role of work in it?

Your Impact Factor

The acts of imagination suggested in Step 1 and in this chapter have one primary purpose — helping you to imagine, and make concrete, the impact that you would like to have through the next phase of your working life. Here are several ways to work that turf.

1. How would you characterize the patterns in the ways you typically exercise impact? For instance: by intervening in problem situations as they arise, by mentoring and supporting people when the need arises, by orchestrating educational experiences for people, by creating policies that stretch people, by trying to be a role model…there are probably many.

2. How do they relate to your answers to the previous question, about how changes you want to see in the world are likely to occur?

3. Of the ways you generally try to have an impact, which ones have historically worked well for you?

4. How can you create more opportunities for these kinds of influence?

5. Which ones have historically backfired?

6. How can you let go of these patterns (or be more selective in their use) and find opportunities for new ways of influencing situations?

7. At the end of your career, what long-term trends of social or environmental change would you most like to be part of?

8. Would you like to be able to say "I protected these five acres and this river-bank" or "I helped replace a seriously toxic chemical with something safer" or "I turned graduating seniors loose on the world with an ability to find their way"?

9. How do you think those changes occur — e.g., by what mix of education, legal advocacy, political pressure, creative inspiration, models that can be imitated?

Take some time to write about the change processes you think are most important in achieving the results you want to see in the world. Now reread what you've written with an eye on the actors: who has done the work to make it happen? And where might you fit?

Listening to the Headlines

This exercise and the next two provide some ways to think about the work to be done in the world. This exercise lets you look from many angles, taking events in the real world as your starting point.

Let any headline catch your eye. Visualize the picture it paints. What does that picture tell you about work that's important? Consider work that's been

Saving farmland gets group thought

Frank Racial Dialogue Thrives on the Web

What can I do for the Rainforest?

New prosperity Brings New Conflict to Indian Country

Hispanic Vote Shapes Up

Feast links Judaism, Christianity

No-mow lawns aren't too far off

Economy Kept Pace

done, to achieve something of value; work that's been neglected or done unwisely, to achieve an unfortunate outcome; work that's emerging as necessary based on events of right now. For example: "Million Man March Stirs Enthusiasm and Debate" says to one person, Community organizing is the work that brought these men together. To another, it says, Psychological and cultural work with men is what made this gathering possible. More of that work needs to be done. To still another, the message may be, Forget about all the sociological stuff. The work to be done is in urban economic redevelopment and venture capital for businesses owned by people of color.

Letter to Future Generations

(Adapted from exercise designed by Joanna Macy)

You actually have an opportunity to send a message to the future, and specifically to young people. How far ahead can you imagine with some concreteness? Ten years, or 200? Whatever era it might be, focus there and let a picture of that world arise in your imagination. Wherever your attention is drawn, let it rest so that details can come into focus. Imagine the dwellings, the streets, the countryside, commerce, how people move from place to place. Watch the adults as they work. Watch the children, wherever you see them.

Let one or more young people draw your attention. In your imagination, turn to them and invite them to listen to you. When you feel ready, begin to tell them what's going on around here today and what kind of impact you would like to have on it through your work. Tell them about the state of the planet today as you see it: what's beautiful and valuable, what's threatened and threatening. Describe your life and the choices about work that you are grappling with. What's the experience of living with these concerns? Finally, tell them how you hope your life will make a difference in the quality of the natural and social environment their generation will inherit. What patterns do you want to change? Who are your allies in this? What forces and individuals get in the way? How would the changes you hope for actually happen? What are you willing to do to have an impact?

The questions and exercises will generate desires and probably some options. You can refine them with a related exercise. Imagine yourself working in any of the fields that come up in the visualization above. Let your imagination expand to include your hypothetical colleagues, mentors, young ones coming in, other enterprises you interact with — the social ecosystem of your work.

What do you imagine this collective enterprise might accomplish? What might they try and fail? In what ways are they (and you) brave and encouraging? In what ways might the collective effort be disappointing? Just sit with the possibilities your imagination brings up; pay attention to what's concrete and rings true for you as a possibility, but don't think too much about what's socially defined as realistic. Homing in on your personal role: Where did you end up? What did you contribute — through the direct impact of your work and its ripple effects?

Which of these scenarios is most exciting? Which is most concrete? Where there is excitement without concreteness, take time to do some more research. Where there is concreteness without excitement, ask what could be done to add juice — or keep the possibility as a backup.

Anchoring Your Values: Three Questions

We have now covered most of the questions that are conventionally considered in a career exploration, and a few others. Now we are going to address a cluster of concerns that mostly come up on people's radar after they've made choices they regret.

1. How do you understand your sense of place and comfort zone with respect to geographic mobility?

It is often assumed that we are infinitely adaptable in choosing where we will live and how. Or, if we aren't, there's something wrong with us. Migrant workers, language teachers, corporate trainers or eco-tour guides — many of us are becoming what a friend calls "global nomads." Understandably so. It is enticing to follow the seasons, rack up cross-cultural experience and follow the kind of customized track — be it fast or slow — that mobility allows. But the costs of this flexibility are becoming clear, even for the moderately mobile, ranging from disrupted families and neglected friendships to a sense of incoherence in working relationships themselves. Part of the countertrend toward "downshifting" is being more discriminating about the choice to pack up and move, or accept a travel-intensive career. Ever so slowly, employers and working people are remembering that we do have a choice about this, and there's much at stake. Roots shape and hone the individual, in the words of poet Wendell Berry, allowing us to grow "whole in the world, at peace and in place." If a more rooted lifestyle were adopted by a significant number of people, even the planet could benefit through reduced fuel use and road building, and because it would be harder for any of us to stay one step ahead of our own bad decisions.

In what ways has geographic mobility enhanced the quality of your working life?

In what ways has it detracted?

What parts of the world do you feel a particular affinity for? Is there a simple answer, or do you live with conflicts?

If you are conflicted about where home is, what steps could you take in the next phase of your career to get closer to resolution?

What kinds of emotional or expressive needs do you sometimes meet through job mobility or frequent travel? What would it take to meet those needs closer to home?

2. *What kinds of tools and technologies would you like to see in use where you work, and what kinds would you prefer to stay away from?*

To question something isn't necessarily to reject it. But tens of thousands of people are now living with injuries — from infertility caused by IUDs to carpal tunnel syndrome — because we did not claim the right to ask tough enough questions about technologies that we interact with intimately and regularly.

In what ways have technologies been a help to you in creating work that reflects your highest values?

In what ways have technologies created barriers in that effort?

How have technologies affected the balance of power between you and various stakeholders you deal with, such as customers, suppliers, management and the public?

Have you ever been in a situation in which a technology "saved" you from labor you wanted to do or skills you wanted to exercise? How did you reconcile that situation? How has the experience shaped your attitudes about technologies and your power to make wise choices in their use?

Have you ever been in a situation in which you were uncomfortable using a technology, but everyone else around you seemed to accept it, so you went along? Looking back, how do you feel about that experience? Is there any other approach you could take if a similar situation arises in the future?

Because it is easy to take technology for granted, here are ten critical perspectives adapted from Jerry Mander's *In the Absence of the Sacred: On the Failure of Technology and the Survival of the Indian Nations* (a brilliant and recommended manifesto whose language I have softened just a little).[8] As you consider the products and services you might be developing, and the technological surround of your work situation, try on the following attitudes:

- Since most of what we are told about technology comes from its proponents, be deeply skeptical of all claims.
- Assume all technology is "guilty until proven innocent."
- Get over the idea that technology is neutral or "value free." Every technology has inherent and identifiable social, political and environmental consequences.
- The fact that technology has a natural flash and appeal is meaningless. Negative attributes are slow to emerge.
- Never judge a technology by the way it benefits you personally. Seek a holistic view of the impacts. Who benefits? Who is at risk? Who decides?
- Keep in mind that individual technology is only one piece of a larger web of technologies. What is the bigger picture that a given technology fits into, in your view?
- Make distinctions between the technologies that primarily serve the individual or the small community and those that operate on a large scale outside community control.
- When it is argued that the benefits of the technological lifeway are worthwhile despite harmful outcomes, recall that Lewis Mumford referred to these alleged benefits as 'bribery.'
- Do not accept the homily "Once the genie is out of the bottle you cannot put it back."
- In the context of widespread technology promotion, do not be afraid to consider the negative. This brings balance.

3. What are your requirements for joy and beauty? (Yes, requirements.) And how will you satisfy them in your working life?

Visiting a colleague some years ago, I was reminded about the lovely moments that can find their way into a workday. We were driving from lunch to her office when she made a sudden multilane change, hooked a left and pulled into a parking lot. "Back in a flash," she said with a smile. "This is my boyfriend's office, and I just want to stop for a quick kiss." Two minutes later we were back on course, with attitudes nicely adjusted.

Walking in beauty does not require a fancy office or other material resources. It's an inside job and a matter of resourcefulness with the materials at hand. One flower in a glass on the desk, or a few fragments of poetry on the wall, can establish a tone. Some employers recognize the value of these "small" amenities, like a full employee refrigerator, and provide them as an investment to keep people happy and effective. Mitch Teplitsky, Director of Marketing for the Film Society of New York, infused his workplace with humanizing touches in this job and others. He brought in a yoga teacher for lunchtime sessions, which over a season became such a magnet that they had to be expanded. He helped co-workers lobby for bicycle racks to make cycling to work easier — and watched with delight as people got the picture that they could organize and ask for something without fomenting a revolution.

James Hillman, ecopsychologist and social philosopher, proposes that one of the major roots of the environmental crisis is a particular kind of numbing — not just separation from the Earth and ecological disruption, but inability to appreciate the beauty that surrounds us. To be anesthetized, he says, is to be cut off from beauty. One of the driving forces in the resurgence of interest in "right livelihood" is a craving for a juicier quality of worklife. This can be a criterion for screening workplaces — or the basis for creating one.

- When and where have you been moved by beauty lately?
- If you could design a fantasy workplace, furnished and decorated to make you glow whenever you walk in, how would it look?
- What are your assumptions about how much beauty and joy are "realistic" on the job? Where do they come from?
- In your choice of vocation and niche, where and how could you create beauty, or preserve it, or make it more democratically available?

Are You an Entrepreneur?

Besides deciding what you should be doing, take the time to consider the mode in which you should be doing it. An entrepreneur is someone who starts and builds initiatives — usually businesses, but also social ventures, movements and initiatives of other kinds. Some people "know" they are — or aren't — entrepreneurs. But some people never fully explore the possibility. Stereotypes get in the way — like the notion that entrepreneurs have to be brilliant, flashy, aggressive or driven. There are many modes. Joline Godfrey, superb trainer of young women to be successful in business, has developed a wonderful assessment in her book, *An Income of Her Own: Women Entrepreneurs Having Fun,*

Making Money, Doing Good. Among the questions: Can you run a dinner party for eight? Do you have good relationships?

There is no magic metric for this decision, but if you are taking a fresh look at your own potential to start and run an enterprise, consider the following categories and get feedback from people who will give you a straight answer.

Vision

Do you have a clear sense of purpose, and can you translate this into the work to be done this year? This month? Tomorrow?

Confidence

Are you generally comfortable with your own decisions on major issues? Can you ask for, and accept, feedback?

Organization

Are you organized without being too buttoned-down? Can you generally find the documents and contact information you need to be productive?

People Skills

Are you good with running meetings, brokering relationships, resolving conflicts, understanding group dynamics? Do others come to you for help in these areas? Do you hold people together socially? Are you good with dinner parties, block parties, coaching teams, parent-teacher association meetings?

Risk

Are you comfortable with risk in general — whether or not you accept a particular one? Do you have a way to calculate risks and benefits in your present circumstances? Do you have an instinct about the degree of risk that is appropriate in the present situation?

Integrity

Do you naturally take stands of integrity and feel uncomfortable when circumstances compromise your ability to do that? Are you skilful at bringing problems to light and addressing them even when it is difficult?

Self-assessment Summary

This structure may help you to gather together and summarize the results of this chapter's exercises.

Because I: I would thrive in workplaces that:

_____   _____

_____   _____

_____   _____

_____   _____

_____   _____

_____   _____

_____   _____

_____   _____

_____   _____

_____   _____

_____   _____

_____   _____

_____   _____

_____   _____

_____   _____

_____   _____

_____   _____

_____   _____

_____   _____

_____   _____

_____   _____

_____   _____

_____   _____

_____   _____

_____   _____

Self-assessment Implications:
Characteristics of an Attractive Workplace

Characteristics of the workplace with regard to:	your comfort zone	stretch zone	no way!
size			
structure			
culture			
tools and technologies			
compensation			
travel and overtime			
location			
flexibility			
ways of enforcing policies and performance			
physical appearance, layout, esthetics			
mix of people in workforce			
possible career paths			
other considerations			

Generating Options

When you have made the best possible sense of your self-assessment and the kinds of working situations where you best fit, it is time to conceive of the actual work options. This means mapping Step 4's opportunities with this step's picture of your strengths and desires.

Get yourself a good-sized piece of paper. Like newsprint. Start thinking up all the options you're entertaining for your work and put them down on the paper any way *except* in a list. You might represent them as a sky full of stars, some of them in constellations together; a tree with branches and twigs; a fanciful collage; or simply related clusters. Stay with the process until you can look at the paper and say, "This completely represents the options I'm interested in exploring."

Review the options you generated. Which ones look like a possible fit based on your exploration so far? Are there any others that don't seem to fit the criteria you've identified, but that still glow mysteriously in your mind and need to be checked out?

You might want to copy this picture, keep the original intact and cut up the copy so that clusters of similar options are kept together, but major categories are separated. This makes it possible to paste each section onto a notebook page, leaving enough blank area to start notes for brainstorming ideas and questions.

Identify which ones are possible now, which ones are longer term and which current possibilities might be stepping stones to the longer-term interests.

For each option or cluster of related options:

1. What do you already know about these areas of work?
2. What do you need to know about these areas of opportunity?
3. What sources do you already know about for gathering this information?

These questions will draw you right back to Step 4 to make a more concrete research plan and begin exploring.

Some of the lines of exploration in this chapter will come alive for you more than others. Please take what's useful and let go of the rest. For the findings that really resonate for you, take time to ask, "So what does this mean for my working life?" The answers may not be obvious.

Eventually, though, the moment will come when self-exploration reaches a natural conclusion for the time being. You will know when this happens. You may feel stale, or restless, or frustrated or simply done. Go forward. When it's time for more self-examination, you will know.

STEP

6

Identify the Essence
of Your Work in the World

*There is a vitality, a life force, an energy, a quickening that is translated
through you into action. And because there is only one of you in all time,
this expression is unique, and if you block it, it will never exist through
any other medium. It will be lost. The world will not have it.
It is not your business to determine how good it is, nor how valuable,
nor how it compares to other expressions. It is your business
to keep the channel open. You do not even have to believe in yourself
or your work. You have to keep aware and open directly to the urges
that activate you. Keep the channel open.*

— Martha Graham[1]

If your workplace burned to the ground and you had to start over, what would
you do? If you distilled all the ingredients of your values and guiding images
and cares for the world into a single drop, how would it taste? If you listed all
the attributes and impacts of your desired work, then one-by-one crossed off
all you could live without, what are the exact words that would still live on the
page? What have been the underlying characteristics or themes of your working life regardless of the jobs you were doing? What have been the primary
roles you have gravitated toward and loved most? What have you found a way
to do in almost any situation? Somewhere in these answers, there is an essential
impulse to action that guides your choices — a gestalt or organizing principle.
It may be well-developed or embryonic, but it will come to life when you begin

to name it and take action on its behalf. As you do this, you take charge of your working life.

Here's an example. One friend of mine started her adult life as a music major and choir director. Then she married and spent some years as a mother and homemaker. As her kids grew, she became more and more active in the community, hosting a TV talk show and getting involved in the civil rights movement. Moving back into paid employment, she joined the field staff for a national non-profit organization concerned with peacemaking. Then she became a fundraiser for another grassroots organization. Through all these shifts, people who have known her for years say she has always done essentially the same work: gathering people together for sociability and celebration, for learning about each other and working together to solve common problems. Issues of widespread concern, from nuclear arms control to family planning, have been focal at times. In every job, she has used superb social skills and a sensitivity to group dynamics. In every job, she has learned a new set of technical skills to do her work in a new way. Whether her overt role is "fundraiser" or "community organizer" or "teacher" or "mother," the essence of her work is building community in a way that gets people participating in social movements.

I've been listening lately to people's simple statements about their work and hearing powerful messages about who they think they are and can be. Craftsperson, communicator, organizer, healer, advocate, technical innovator, marketer and builder are one-word descriptions that speak volumes, not only about the specific job but about the values and priorities that animate it. Many career counselors advise a slightly more detailed, but still simple, descriptive statement, not only for self-definition but for self-promotion as well:

- I'm a teacher with international experience who really wants to see a new kind of intercultural program in our school system.
- I'm an engineer with ten years experience in transportation systems, and I want to help small to medium-sized cities design mass transit systems that work.
- And this from the manager of the computer department for a small non-profit organization, only half kidding: I'm the guy who does everything around here that doesn't require social skills.

Fundraising expert Laurie Blum draws attention to her books and consulting services with the title *Free Money*. Author and seminar leader Barbara Winter supports self-employed people she calls the "joyfully jobless."[2] A tailoring service caught my eye with the name "Clothes Clinic." Attorney Kimm Walton syndicates her well-researched column on legal careers in more than 300 outlets by proclaiming herself, "The Job Goddess."

Naming focuses the nature of your work and its market. Maria DuBois was only sure that her role involved some kind of information exchange in the realm of health services until the term "healthcare broker" crystallized in her mind; what she does is help people navigate through the maze of specialties and the dilemmas regarding alternative care, make wise choices, identify providers, evaluate costs and line up regimens of care without making themselves sicker in the process. Entrepreneurs get to choose what to call themselves. Some companies conspire with employees to create interesting and informative job titles — like the Endangered Species Chocolate Company, where the webmaster and designer is called Director of Intelligence and the Director of Finance doubles as Director of Defense.

Beyond its focusing and marketing value, the ritual of naming can have an enormous mythic impact on the person who accepts it and internalizes its meaning. John Cronin grew up on the Hudson River near New York City and tried on many identities for protecting the waters, including several years as an aide in the New York State Assembly. Eventually, in the 1970s, he let himself be persuaded to work for a minimal salary patrolling the river in a small boat, representing an embryonic non-profit organization with a bold name, "The Riverkeeper." In his 1998 memoir co-authored with partner Robert Kennedy Jr., *The Riverkeepers*, he vividly remembers the moment his resolve was first tested. He encountered a huge barge discharging a large quantity of something unknown into the river. "Who goes there?" he demanded with megaphone in hand. The Exxon Corporation identified itself. "And who goes there?" came the counter-question. From somewhere in Cronin's being came the authority to shout out, "The Riverkeeper." His documentation of this discharge, and many more, contributed to the successful prosecution of the polluters. The Riverkeeper became a legal advocacy project of some sophistication and quickly sent a message that the Hudson River was no longer a place to take illegal wastes "away." Riverkeepers, mountainkeepers and other watchdog organizations using this model have sprung up by the dozens across the country.

This individual step — taking full responsibility for naming what you have to offer and why it matters — fits interestingly with the evolution of business into a more knowledge-intensive realm. Many of the best employers are recognizing that one of the primary factors that can distinguish them in the marketplace is the knowledge and human talents they hold uniquely. Intellectual capital is valued as never before because it creates innovation as well as anticipating and dealing with risk and responsibility. Individual and organizational knowledge — and the ability to mobilize that knowledge effectively — is so important because it differentiates an organization from others. As professor Michael Porter points out, "A company can outperform rivals only if it can establish a difference that it can preserve. Competitive strategy is about being different. It means deliberately choosing a different set of activities to deliver a unique mix of value."[3]

Simply put, cookie-cutter workplaces need cookie-cutter people, but distinctive workplaces are recognizing the need for distinctive people.

Some people find it helpful to think about these capsule descriptions in terms of personal "mission." This seems to work best when it comes from within, authentically and easily, and when it's held lightly. If romanticized or taken up uncritically, a sense of mission can also provide an escape hatch from the mundane but necessary day-to-day questions about how to live. It can lead to fanaticism, inflexibility and unrealistic expectations for staying on a single track. As Rick Jarow observes, "Many people who are absolutely sure of what they want to do with their lives are clinically crazy."

Lots of people think there is an automatic fit between qualities they see in themselves and kinds of work they could do. They think that self-assessment and investigation of the options, by themselves, will force a choice to pop out. Choosing work is not a logical activity; it's an informed gamble as to which of the available possibilities will really draw the most from you.

This process of discrimination comes to life when you identify two aspects of your work:

- The essence or core ("What's necessary if I'm going to be myself with integrity in my work?") and
- The limits you need to set to work with integrity ("What's not okay for me — what's an unacceptable compromise or a violation of my values — in my choice and performance of work?").

These are two complementary ways of asking, "What conditions do I need to hold out for in my work if I want to be able to look at myself in the mirror in the morning?" You may not always be able to meet those conditions. But you can keep them in mind, put your antenna out for new approaches to the search and give yourself permission to keep asking whether a particular compromise position is still necessary. That questioning process often uncovers assumptions that are unnecessarily restrictive. A client of mine with fabulous administrative and financial management skills struggled, for a time, about whether or not to admit to prospective employers that she had gained these skills by living on a large ashram. Eventually her attention was drawn to the discomfort she felt in the interviews when glossing over this most important part of her history, which still shaped her spiritual life. She wondered how comfortable it would be to go to work every day and be apprehensive about disclosing this part of her history to co-workers. Exploring the options for talking about it, she got clear that:

1. Those years had been a rich time of professional development because they had involved so much collaborative decision-making, cross-training with co-workers and implementing the techniques of stress management and conflict management they were teaching others, years before they gained common currency.

2. Potential employers who had no experience with ashrams might have legitimate questions about her experience — for example, how she would fit into the workplace culture — and she could demonstrate her communication skills and proactive stance by shifting her role in the interview subtly from "applicant" to "educator."

3. She could transform the situation with warmth, humor and fearlessness.

Even if your sense of personal purpose is quite general, you are still operating within an ethical framework and can still benefit from making it explicit, first and foremost to yourself. One approach to this is illustrated by my friend Steve Kropper, the CEO of a Boston information business called Inpho that helps prospective homebuyers find out about neighborhood property values and other factors that might influence their buying decisions. Having more than paid his dues in the world of high risk — running innovative energy conservation businesses in the 1980s and surfing several turbulent waves of governmental funding — Steve rediscovered the value of having time for a marriage and family and decided that the content of his next business was less important than its ability to create a platform for viable lives for his workforce and a climate where people could learn to value themselves. He entered a stage of life where what mattered most was the immediate: the ability to give excellent training and mentoring to quality employees, to create a nondiscriminatory environment and to have time on the side to take his Cub Scouts out on environmental projects. Steve created a matrix for evaluating job opportunities when he was working for other people; it can also guide him in business opportunities today. It has two dimensions: a company's growth and its impact.

HIGH GROWTH / POSITIVE IMPACT	**HIGH GROWTH / NEGATIVE IMPACT**
LOW GROWTH / POSITIVE IMPACT	**LOW GROWTH / NEGATIVE IMPACT**

Steve explains:

I figure that a growing enterprise will be best able to afford to be generous, both with opportunities for me and in letting me use my position to do good for other people. So I look for businesses that are growing. They also have to be at least neutral and preferably positive in their impact, as I see it. I won't work in a company I think is doing harm, no matter how much it's growing. I'll work in a place where the impact is lukewarm, if the business is expanding and the culture allows me, personally, to have a positive effect through my work. That formula is simple enough that I can put it into practice and still find work. And it generally keeps me out of big trouble.

When you are interested in more than minimizing harm in accomplishing a particular purpose, it becomes all the more important to sift through your options and images of playing them out, until a sense of honest purpose crystallizes. Consider what different paths can be traveled by people using a superficially similar set of skills in service of similar values — and why the particulars of a situation make all the difference. Here are two stories of people with similar skill sets. Both would call themselves designers. But they have each evolved quite different and distinctive bodies of work. For each of them, the distinctive aspect is not the skills being used, but the organizing vision and strategy that guides the use of the skills. Both illustrate the kind of evolutionary process that comes into play as people hone their definition of their own work through practice. Wendy Brawer helps cities and other large groups of people develop "green maps" of environmental assets and damages. Brawer graduated from art school in Seattle in the 1970s, with a major interest in design. She gravitated to the field of industrial design, that is, designing things that are mass-produced, "one of the most flexible of design fields." Although resource-efficiency naturally attracted her, she did not consider herself an environmentalist beyond that. But she couldn't help but take notice of the turbulence throughout the community as Seattle's major industry, Boeing, was coming apart. The common slogan was "Last one to leave Seattle turn out the lights." Brawer left, for Tokyo, with the aim of making money by teaching English and making sure her life didn't grow dull.

Two experiences, together, got her attention: getting involved in an artistic collaboration on a "countdown to the millennium" clock and taking a vacation in Bali. As she reflected:

> Here you are in this absolutely gorgeous place and you come out of your cabin one morning and find a swath of landscape just razed and another guest cabin put on it. People who always walked or rode a bike are suddenly on a scooter. These were things I could see in two weeks.

The combination forced the question, "What am I doing wasting my time?" and she resolved to redirect her life to do as much as possible to protect the environment.

Back in the US, Brawer's design focus led her to think hard about materials use — not only substitution and reduction, but the size of the stream of manufactured goods she saw. "People are drowning in stuff, and here I am helping to produce more stuff for them," she lamented. Professionally, she learned all she could about alternative materials and more streamlined approaches to design. On the side, she got involved in an ambitious campaign, Stamp Out Junk Mail, ultimately sending free information to hundreds of agencies, from state attorneys general's offices out to the grassroots. This was satisfying, but not income-producing. She got funding and did several high-visibility educational projects in waste reduction, including a major display to encourage recycling in Times Square and a waste-reduction project in a housing complex that helped 1,700 apartments each cut water use by 65 gallons a day. This was moving in the right direction, but still felt reactive.

Brawer also began teaching at Cooper Union, blending regular industrial design with "Design for the Environment." While she knew that New York was "a tough city to capture people's imagination," it captured hers. By 1992, when large numbers of delegates to the United Nations Earth Summit were descending on the city, Brawer had figured out that they would want to find the health food stores and parks. That led her to propose and spearhead the production of the first Green Apple Map, giving birth to a Green Map system that now involves 70 municipalities in 20 countries. The New York City map uses a simple system of icons to represent 700 sites including community gardens, coastal wetlands, nature trails, green businesses and recycling centers. Still supplementing her income by teaching, she lives and works in a Soho loft that is the nerve center of Modern World Design, the non-profit that helps communities from Adelaide to Berkeley in conceiving and carrying out their green mapping projects. Like many good designs, the idea was evolutionary rather than preconceived. But it's ecological and educational on many levels, she explains: "Maps are very resource-efficient, they're universally understood and they encourage discovery."

Ken Geiser founded the Massachusetts Toxics Use Reduction Institute, which helps industrial companies in planning and implementing pollution prevention systems. Geiser was trained as an architect and came of age in the extended community orbiting around Frank Lloyd Wright. He has this to say about the path into his current work, which on the surface is far from architecture:

> I didn't intend to do anything like what I'm doing. However, I've always had a huge commitment to social justice and community rights. As I became more involved in civil rights and antiwar work in the 1960s, my commitment to architecture became very complicated, and I left it after two years.
>
> I went to MIT to study urban planning and did a lot of grassroots organizing there. I helped stop a highway. I helped set up a home-based school. I had a growing interest in the environment and working-class life. That drew me into working with trade unions and into a kind of

working-class environmentalism — a notion that, in those days, made no sense at all.

By my early 30s, I had begun, seriously, to find out what my work was. I realized that jobs and projects were ancillary to the work. They were a means of getting the work done. For me, "the work" meant saving us from annihilating ourselves, whether that meant focusing on urban rats or on racial injustices in exposure to environmental hazards — whatever the specifics. Toxic chemicals became my primary vehicle, because that was the most ripe area for organizing.

Geiser spent years integrating an awareness of the condition of human society into his life and identifying different approaches for doing something useful. He had a strong, but general, commitment to the greater good, but was able to entertain many different ideas about how to serve that good. Over the years, through action on his commitment and a whole lot of paying attention, he fine-tuned his views about how to do the work. An unorthodox but powerful organizing principle came to him after a few years in the fray:

I realized that I needed to code this thing in a new way, so to speak. Jokingly at first, and then more seriously, I said I needed a metric for measuring what I was achieving, so that I would be able to take stock at the end of my life.

I chose one that seemed rather silly, but that I've actually taken to heart. I've developed a list of toxic chemicals that are generally agreed to be environmental health hazards of a very significant magnitude. I've decided that the world isn't big enough for them and me. So they have to go. I have dedicated myself to the removal of this series of chemicals from commerce. That way, I can mark my success not only in terms of this passion, but also in very clear behavioral terms.

In the short run, this journey took him out of the profession he loved. But lately, he has come around, full-circle, to new possibilities in using his design training and sensibilities. Now they are directed toward finding new, non-toxic materials for building and industry, articulating the issues in a book called *Materials Matter*, and understanding how industrial decision-makers choose their materials in the first place in order to "tap the most creative forces in the society for building a much better house in the future," metaphorically and literally.

This illustrates a common experience among people who allow themselves to be led by an unfolding sense of purpose and who — within the limits of real-world alternatives at any given time — do their best to choose jobs that help them do "their work." New ideas and images come and are integrated sooner or later. Obsolete understandings are shed. It is not a process any of us can control. We can only pay attention and use what we know about ourselves to shape our strategies, holding onto as many elements as we can and letting go when we have to. Somehow, doing that can lead us back to new ways to make use of the experiences and commitments with which we started out.

Your story doesn't want to be constricted. And when your working life is on track, you feel present to it in a way that makes use of more dimensions of you than you can possibly fit on a page. That is why résumé writing is so annoying and so rewarding. The wizardry of crafting a worthwhile working life starts with using all the resources available to you, including your history, rough spots and all.

Sometimes that essence comes to life more clearly in the moment that you tell another person how you see it. Maureen Hart, a research analyst on measurement systems for sustainable development, tells this story of self-discovery:

> I started as a data geek, and now I recognize that I'm a data poet. What I like to do is take huge quantities of numbers and figure out what they mean. The sort of thing that makes some people's eyes glaze over, I like to look through and ask what the trends are, what I think it means, what's missing. I learned that I have a skill in taking those numbers and boiling it down into a picture that will help people understand what they mean — in the same way that poets boil down relatively few words. I realized I was a poet when I was describing what I do to an English teacher, and he said "that sounds like poetry."

The experience of finding your personal essence, or center, can be profoundly satisfying and sometimes simple. Margaret Burnham, a co-founder of the first African-American women's law firm in Boston, has had a rich and varied career as a lawyer, judge, mother, teacher and community activist. Through it all, her choices have revolved around the moral center established in the moment when her life first turned toward the law.

> I was a teenager in Mississippi in 1964, passing out leaflets in Jackson. A police officer took a leaflet and rounded me up as an illegal demonstra-

tor. I was sitting in jail, contemplating my existence, when a woman showed up. She was my lawyer. I had never seen a lawyer, much less a black woman lawyer. I said to myself, "This has got to be magic."

Certain experiences become guiding metaphors for our lives and work. In Burnham's case, it has been about "living as part of the freedom movement," whatever form that takes. Her early trials connected her to her inner power and helped her to define herself through its symbolism. As Burnham puts it, "That time set up the canvas on which I have painted my life."

Identifying the essence of your work-in-the-world is not a single step but a process. It is about digging deep and continuously reweaving this biographical narrative into the tapestry you want your life to be. Some crystallizing moments are the aha experiences of life, sources of the insight and healing so memorable that you want others to know them firsthand. Many of the moments that help crystallize career directions have to do with our own healing and development. As Burnham's story shows, people or experiences that throw us a lifeline have a special way of capturing our attention with a sense of new possibility. This is also true when we're mired in a set of circumstances that aren't quite working. Will Fudeman, now an acupuncturist and counselor, recalls the sequence of events that led him to focus on a single organizing principle for a career that had been rich but scattered:

> I had three great jobs. I was a therapist part-time. I worked in an educational non-profit part-time. I was a Sunday School program director. On top of that, I played in a Klezmer band. And I was saying to myself, "What do I want to be when I grow up?"
>
> In fact, I said this to myself at great length at two in the morning, when I should have been sleeping. Now, you can give me the obvious response, that I was doing too much and my body was out of balance. But I've been overcommitted before, and this restlessness was new.
>
> I've studied a lot about the immune system and the energies of the body. I took myself to my acupuncturist, who told me I've got a yin deficiency — too much fire in the head. Whatever else that may mean, it meant I got to lie there with needles in me for half an hour, which made me feel a lot more grounded. The worries of my life didn't go away, but I'm better able to deal with them.

Fudeman took that healing potential to heart by becoming a licensed acupuncturist with a practice in oriental medicine in Ithaca and Syracuse, New York. Bringing a perspective on mental health and community issues to his work, he soon developed a specialty consulting with mental health professionals, helping people cut their dependency on prescription drugs for managing pain.

One of the powerful driving forces in adult development, including career development, is the quest for internal consistency, or at least coherence, between what we profess to believe and what we live out. That doesn't mean we can't multi-task, but that it's beneficial to be clear on what's at the center of our interests and concerns. We differ vastly in our comfort zones regarding consistency and in the options handed to us to work with. But leaps forward tend to take place when we can ask challenging questions about the contradictions in our working lives and the resources we have to work with in transcending them.

- Are you leading multiple lives?
- If so, what are the benefits and costs of this?
- What areas of overlap do you see between your career and other "lives" you lead?
- What tensions?
- What might you want to do to more fully integrate your "lives" and expand your choices?

If some aha! moments are connected with healing and insight, other gems to be mined are the ambiguous moments and dark times whose memories can put up barriers to forward movement until they are faced. Some of the finest gems may come directly from darker times in your history. The most uncomfortable situations in your work history are often the ones in which you are forced to face yourself and take stock of your values. The catalyst may have been pressures, ethical dilemmas or obvious mismatches between you and the work situation. Times of difficulty on the job are often times of major learning about the conditions we need in order to work sanely and productively and about the ways we fail ourselves by accepting unacceptable conditions. Ken Geiser, whose career evolved from architecture into a different kind of ecological design, reflects:

> The losses that I've suffered have tended to be some of the best material I've gotten to work with. It took me a long time to realize that the things I was losing were really kicking me along in a way that was very, very

powerful. It's all in the perception you have of yourself, and your ability to hold some things steady even as others change. If you start thinking there's a grand plan — and then you discover that architecture is not going to satisfy you, and the wife that you have is going to leave you, and suddenly you have this collapsed image of yourself — you have to say, "I guess I was wrong. I'm going to have to start over."

If it weren't for those external pushes, it might have been much harder for Geiser to let go of comforts at times, in order to say yes to challenges. Like many people who feel they have found their life's work, he is continually coming to terms with its high demands. "I never intended to have this kind of life," he admits. "For years, I constantly looked for it to flatten out and become normalized." That hasn't happened, but he has learned a lot about self-preservation and the sanctity of the weekend.

Unless he is forced to do so, Geiser does not abandon one set of self-images or goals when others come into focus. He thinks the way a designer does in his work to promote the use of less toxic materials. When necessary, though, he can draw on talents cultivated over the decades, from administration to lobbying to community organizing. He explains:

> I've always brought themes forward from each era in my life. I think that's really critical. We're like books, and the first chapter shouldn't be forgotten. There are metaphors and reasons that come from those early experiences that help make sense of what comes later. One of my models early on was Nat Owings, founder of one of the biggest architectural firms in the country. In his late 40s, he and four other guys walked away from an office in Chicago that they were in trouble over. They all uprooted themselves and went to San Francisco to start over. I always thought, "Well, that's very romantic — but foolish." In my mind, you don't throw out what you've learned. You are one person. You might as well bring the lessons forward. Actually, it has a lot to do with one's respect for oneself, belief in oneself and, quite frankly, love for oneself.

This is not to suggest that every personal breakthrough requires a career reassessment, or that it's necessary to have made complete peace with your history before moving on the work front. In fact, the opposite can be true. Moving forward with career choices, especially challenging ones, can be a source of rich revelation about who you are and what you need. For many people, a handful of crystallizing experiences like the ones we've been discussing provide enough material for a life's worth of career development. Looking at insights from personal work history in some depth can sometimes bring obvious connections to light between insults and struggles in the past, and perceived limitations in the present. At times, too, dipping into those painful memories can bring unexpected reassurance. Experiences that seemed like pure failure can take on a very different meaning with time.

For example, early in her career, Rose Diamond was a secretary, mother of three and part-time college student in North Carolina. She could not have predicted the sequence of events that would lead her, over a dozen years, to be training as an art educator in Boston. Diamond had only a faint sense of what was ahead — a fascination with the arts, a drive for more education and an exploring nature. Her memory of that era illustrates the way many of us really move our lives forward — by leaping into opportunities that are somehow compelling, even if we are not always able to make full use of them right away:

> I had always wanted to work in radio, and they were just starting up a National Public Radio station in Charlotte. I went in and volunteered. I had an idea for a huge project: a storytelling show for children. Storytelling was just starting to come back into the culture, and there were wonderful mountain stories. My son's friend's father was a great storyteller. I got the go-ahead to get a pilot show together and apply for funding from IBM.
>
> I had never done anything like this before. I was scared to death. But I went ahead. I developed the proposal. I got the story recorded. And then I went to do an interview with a local literature professor whose backing we needed. I took my tape recorder but pushed the wrong buttons. We did an hour-long interview. But when I went to play it back, there was nothing there. I got so scared. I thought, "There's no way I'm going to make this happen." I backed out, and I was so embarrassed that I didn't follow through for years.

During those years, Diamond put one foot in front of the other to keep her children fed and uncover more of her skills and strengths. She finished college with a major in art history and museum studies. Her marriage ended. She worked for a time in a museum. Then, disabled by a car accident, she was forced into an entirely different rhythm of living for many months: resting, physical therapy and days that were wide open for writing or drawing or working with clay. During her convalescence, she was showered with attention by co-workers in a way that profoundly increased her own self-esteem. Eventually she was able to say, "I guess I'm an artist," and, some time later, "I suppose I could be a good teacher." No single event led to either of those acknowledgments; they grew organically out of the life she was leading and her openness to new images of herself.

Curiosity drew her to a more urban setting. Moving to Boston, she found her way into a small graduate school whose programs integrate the arts and education. By coincidence, the college was home to a national center for oral history and storytelling, bringing her around full circle to that earlier interest. Viewing the potential and unknowns at the beginning of the program, she was able to say,

> I'm finally going to find out where Rose's creativity is. For the first time in my life I'm able to take the risk and not worry, just take one hurdle at a time. Since I've stopped to pay attention to my inner life, I don't have the need to be an overachiever anymore, so I'm much more free to act. I know now that I wasn't ready, back in 1980, to do that public radio show. My self-esteem wasn't high enough. That's why I quit.

These cycles of incubation and expression are essential to evolution for many people. Often a shift from one phase to another is triggered by a crystallizing moment that pulls diverse puzzle pieces together. Consultant Judy Otto describes a slow evolution of her professional focus, from industry to healthcare, during a period when friends of hers were facing life-threatening illnesses and the healthcare crisis was becoming national news. Those events brought numerous possibilities into her mind, but at first they did not easily translate into a course of action. She was able to coast. One day, though, she was struck by a line of poetry by Antonio Machado: "What will you do with this garden that has been entrusted you?" She knew it was time to act, simply by directing her marketing efforts toward the clients she most wanted to help rather than waiting for business to come in the door.

In finding the gems in your experience that will help you to value your work fully and accurately, one of the most important processes is learning to see yourself in an evolutionary sense — that is, to assimilate actual changes into your subjective image of yourself, rather than hanging onto outdated aspects of your self-image. If you take this for granted, consider yourself lucky. Without the skill of continuous reassessment, new experiences don't become part of your evolving self-image; you may test and prove yourself endlessly because you've never paused to notice real accomplishments; you may find yourself stuck, at midlife, in the self-image of a beginner.

One of the most important kinds of experience to assess, when you are in the midst of a transition, is how and where you've actually moved in the most recent phase of life, just in case your self-image hasn't completely kept up with events. Here are some questions for taking stock of where you stand in a time of job transition:

1. How have you grown in your present or last work situation?
2. What did you set out to accomplish, personally and professionally, in this role?
3. In what ways did you accomplish these things? What accomplishments are you most proud of?
4. How do these suggest new areas of responsibility, and new sources of marketability, for you in the future?
5. What were you most appreciated for on the job and by whom?
6. What strengths of yours were not given the acknowledgment they deserved, and how has that fact shaped your ability to move into the next phase with confidence?
7. What were your characteristic struggles on the job?
8. In what ways were these a reflection of the work environment, and in what ways were they a reflection of your style and psychological needs in the situation?
9. What did you learn from those struggles that could help you to achieve the same goals with less suffering? What might you still need to learn or articulate, in order to feel complete?

A healthy sense of purpose comes from the land of the living. That is, it arises through engagement with people, communities and nature, in the course of trying to do even a little something useful. You learn that you are a nurturer by working for a community agency teaching handicapped people how to garden. The garden is threatened by a highway right-of-way, and you discover overnight that you're also a fighter. You learn about the untapped reservoirs of community support when people come out and get involved. You learn about betrayal, during the court battle, when your agency becomes factionalized. Over the years, your sense of professional identity and direction grows a lot like the garden. It gets less idealized and more personalized. You are challenged to make peace with overlapping and conflicting loyalties in terms of who you really work for: the clients who benefit from the garden directly, the agency that oversees it and helps many others, the vision of urban gardening…or hands-on education…or land preservation. You know the kind of soil you need to work productively and the kinds of fruits your labor can produce. You refine this understanding as you move forward, through small choices and larger ones, identifying the essence *right now* and then further refining it through each action you take.

Commit Yourself to Doing Your Work in Some Form, Whether or Not Anyone Is Paying You for It Right Now

This is not work for the timid of heart.
The benefits of it are immeasurable.
Yet it requires personal struggle.
Only when you change internally will you see
those benefits reflected in the outside world.
You have to go through a process, and it's painful.
You have to show up fearlessly.

RICHARD BARRETT[1]

From Essence to Action

Start with your definition of "what's essential." Now consider: what actions toward that vision are totally within your power? What can you do, beginning now? And what, in particular, could you commit yourself to, that would place you in the stream of "your work" for real, now, without waiting for anyone's permission? What kinds of support would you need to pull them off? How would you need to "grow yourself" as a human being to sustain these commitments? Of the choices of commitments before you, which one(s) would be the most powerful?

This chapter focuses on the inner process of commitment and the ways to animate and guide it. The next chapter focuses on the action steps that are then possible, and some strategies for translating commitment specifically into employment. But first, some images of possibility.

Listen to George Bliss, as he worked to commercialize bicycle-powered pedicabs as a transportation alternative in New York City. As he admitted:

New York is the hardest place in the world for getting this idea to work. New Yorkers are very prone to lawsuits, very jumpy about insurance issues. Storage space is at a premium. And there are no institutions that have a stake in seeing locally produced alternative vehicles. So I figure that if I can get it to work here, it can work anywhere.

Listen to Paula Gutlove, director of the Balkans Peace Project, a team of mediators and trainers who visited areas outside the war zones of the former Yugoslavia to train community leaders in conflict resolution methods, hoping to prevent new explosions of violence:

> I'll get into the taxi to go to the airport for these mammoth journeys, with one of my kids clinging to each leg saying "Don't leave." I'll get into the taxi asking "Why am I doing this? This is insane. I don't want to go." I meet up with my colleagues, who are saying the same things. Then, after the workshop, we know why we're doing it. Bringing together a group of people from different ethnic backgrounds and having them hear each other — that's success for me.

In these cases and many more, the source of commitment is decidedly larger than the individual's narrow self-interest. Difficult paths are accepted and even embraced because they are connected to a large enough purpose — sometimes larger than the individual can figure out in the moment. Some of us may think we are literally a channel for a purpose larger than ourselves. Sharon Welch, theologian and women's studies professor, reminds us that in many cultures this is an ordinary mode of operation. It is a fairly rare luxury to be able to hold change at arm's length and choose only those risks that have clear payoffs. People holding a large measure of social power can do this; most of us, most of the time, need to unlearn the expectation, especially if we are working on behalf of projects or interests that are part of a new order rather than the entrenched one. In *A Feminist Ethic of Risk*, Welch tells the stories of African-American women in positions of leadership in the civil rights movement.[2] Consistently, they took action, not when the risk was necessarily low or the payoff clear, but when the need was pronounced. Paradoxically, as they let go of controlling the results, their actions had impacts that reverberated far beyond their conscious vision. The letting-go occurred in the context of commitment to a vision larger than personal hopes or outcomes.

Psychologist and educator Laura Sewall reflects that one of the most common barriers to commitment is actually ego, "wanting to wait and see, wanting to keep those old options open." As a consequence, one of the best ways into a healthy commitment is not the exertion of will, but a kind of surrender to the logic of the situation. Gwendolyn Hallsmith, a planner and community development facilitator who has played key roles in community turnarounds from South Africa to Canada, expresses the way that love of work and love of life can feed each other:

> It has always helped me to have a regular, deepening spiritual practice. When you are centered and regularly practice meditation, prayer and silence it does not feel very often like the universe is conspiring against you. On the contrary — I think that the universe is primarily responsible for the energy and commitment I do have. I just try not to fight it and let it happen. It helps to recognize serendipity and synchronicity when they come your way and be flexible enough to follow your heart. Even though I think that things like mission statements and strategic plans are important, in some ways precisely because they set an intention for your efforts, you can't always plan your way into situations where you'll have the opportunities you need to have a real impact.

As these examples show, healthy commitment comes from within. It offers a path for self-expression and actualization. It may require deferring gratification in significant ways, but it doesn't require stuffing down your essential self. It is not about self-sacrifice, but about self-expression, about uncovering a personal vision and steadily directing inner and outer resources toward bringing that vision alive. Naturally enough, when that vision is capable of touching other lives, leaving a legacy or changing the conditions around you, its attractive force can be especially strong.

Commitment requires connection. You can't play the oboe part of a symphony alone onstage. You can't be a literacy teacher if there's nobody there to learn from you. But you can offer demonstrations, attract collaborators, write proposals and business plans, give talks, volunteer a little time to assist people who are noted in the field and otherwise take action that will strengthen your connections and credibility — all while waiting and watching for a more formal opportunity. Doing so will rarely hurt in attracting that opportunity.

Unconditional commitment is not the same as addictive attachment. You can be totally committed to your work while continuing to exercise critical judgment about acceptable means for doing it. No matter how much you want to gain experience in corporate communications, for instance, you may decide against volunteering your labor for a profitable company that has just laid off some of your neighbors. But you might design an internship with them and seek out a scholarship fund that would pay you a stipend. On the other hand, you might prefer to learn the same skills by proposing an internship with the outplacement firm that's helping those laid-off workers find other jobs, or with an agency concerned with economic development or with a community group fighting to save jobs. In most situations, there are multiple paths to the same goal.

Commitment to doing *your* work, whether or not you're being paid, does not mean giving up on making a living at your chosen work eventually. This is an especially important point for people who have been giving it away for too long. The spirit of healthy, self-affirming commitment means discovering the kinds of actions that let you move toward a goal with satisfaction and even joy, so that commitment to work and commitment to personal well-being coincide as often as possible. As Marsha Sinetar expresses it,

> When we are pursuing our Right Livelihood, even the most difficult and demanding aspects of our work will not sway us from our course. When others say, "Don't work so hard" or "Don't you ever take a break?" we will respond in bewilderment. What others may see as duty, pressure, or tedium we perceive as a kind of pleasure. Commitment is easy when our work is Right Livelihood.

Meditators and athletes know the concept of practice, and that concept applies to any field of endeavor. In the words of writer and writing teacher Natalie Goldberg,

> I told my writing students that practice is something done under all circumstances, whether you're happy or sad. You don't become tossed away by a high weekend or a blue Monday. Writing is something you do quietly, regularly, and in doing it, you face your life.[3]

One growing support system for commitment to work that makes the world a better place is the international Graduation Pledge Alliance, based at Bentley College and with hundreds of participating campuses and thousands of pledgers across North America and Asia.[4] In fact, the particular flavor of enlightened work ethic that is reflected in these pages came to life in part because of a phone call from a Pledge founder, Matt Nicodemus, asking for resources to help pledgers follow through on their commitment, at a time when those resources were few. Pledge campaigns are gentle opportunities for graduates to affirm to their peers that they will thoroughly investigate the social and environmental responsibility of any employment they consider. Campaigns, initiated by students or faculty, generally start with programming to familiarize students with the issues and promote exploration.

Graduates report a variety of impacts as their careers evolve. Chemist Christine Miller found her first job in a company whose name contained the word "environmental." But before long she chanced to be part of a water-cooler conversation in which her boss asked her opinion about a potential contract involving something too toxic to meet her approval. She expressed her opinion. Her boss approached her later and said, "We've decided not to go for that contract." Heartened, Miller nevertheless found herself more and more attentive to the health, safety and environmental issues around her. She grew less and less comfortable with her job and finally sought out another. Thanks to the Pledge, she is now happier, working as a chemist for Abbott Laboratories, developing infant formulas and nutritional products.

"OK," you say, "I'm committed...but to what?" It might be to a long-range vision, whether or not many details of getting there are clear. Your commitment might be to working with a population or region or species or issue, although your roles and specific interests may evolve greatly. Your commitment might be to finding a way to participate in an election or campaign by the time it is launched: you might use this as a challenge and try out everything from phone banking to speech writing as a possible mode for carrying out the commitment. Of course, you might find that the most important thing to be committed to is a healthy process of moving forward, in the spirit of a client of mine who responded to the exercise below with the pledge: "Every week, I commit myself to spending at least one hour a week *not* obsessing on finding work."

Two Models

The approaches to the challenge of coherent, life-sustaining commitment are infinite. But they all build on two basic economic modes: the volunteer and the entrepreneur.

A volunteer works without pay — but not necessarily without a role, respect and other forms of compensation. Volunteers are not all envelope-stuffers. Some serve on boards of directors. Others are strategic advisors, speechwriters, computer helpers, canvass directors, project managers and more.

Entrepreneurs are not all lean-and-hungry marketeers. They may be piano teachers or acupuncturists. Some build up their practices through word of mouth in a single community, while others work by mail order or computer network on a national or even international scale.

Barbara Winter, a trainer and chronicler of the "joyfully jobless," reflects:

> People are becoming self-employed because their self-esteem is in good order and they want to learn more about what they can be as human beings. For a lot of them, that's connected to a vision of a different kind of world they'd like to build. I see this as the most powerful force in entrepreneurship and a tremendous source of commitment. It makes things like driving an eight-year-old car or working on weekends seem really unimportant.

By accepting full responsibility for launching your work in this spirit, you are reclaiming the initiative, powerfully. You're shifting the focus onto the emerging possibilities, cultivating will and clarity. You're building up skills. You are also presenting yourself to the world as a doer, not a "want-to-be." This shift can be mirrored in your self-image. It is a guaranteed way to stand out, to learn fast and to attract all kinds of support that can help move you toward your goal. There is no better way to get to know leaders, innovators and other allies in the field, increasing your access to information about ways to do your work for pay. And especially if your efforts help to create or fund a new project, you may be literally helping to create your own position.

Environmental consultant Simon Gruber illustrates the path of commitment with flexibility and enjoyment, through a life of energy education and advocacy, watershed protection work and more. He reflects on the access and impact you can create with "soft" skills while feeling your way into the specific opportunities ahead:

> It's worked for me to volunteer for committees, projects and so on, as a way of meeting people, learning about issues and being in the right place at the right time when some kind of paying work opportunity arises. If you're interested in working on an issue or starting a project,

try organizing an educational workshop. You don't have to be an expert to bring in experts and organize successful events. If you are a good writer, use these skills to write proposals, seek grants, etc. and/or write articles about issues and organizations you are interested in. If you are not a good writer, practice this crucial skill. Don't be shy about calling, writing, e-mailing or walking up to people to talk. It can be useful to ask a question you already know the answer to, just to get things going, and you may learn something unexpected.

Learn to listen well. Most people are more interested in telling you what they know or about themselves, than they are in hearing your story. If there's someone you want to get to know, listen to them carefully and then discuss your interests in a context that fits with theirs. Don't underestimate the importance of your contacts and your network — people you meet today may be in a position to help you a year from now, or 20 years from now, if you can maintain a good working relationship. It goes without saying that you need to be courteous and gracious always.

At the risk of sounding crass, I know of no better network for cultivating job and project opportunities than a social movement. Movements unite people and provide great networks of individuals who share your values and may well want to support you by sharing resources and contacts. Veteran activists often relate to each other with high levels of trust, a common ethical culture and a history of cooperating in the name of a larger goal. Of course, this works only if you are authentically involved in a movement and have shown your commitment in tangible ways, not if you are cruising it for contacts.

People who become truly caught up in making something happen often work as a volunteer and an entrepreneur at the same time. They do whatever is needed to keep the work going. In more everyday situations, you have the luxury of thinking ahead about which image, the volunteer or the entrepreneur, will be your best organizing principle. Both orientations require high levels of initiative and commitment. But both can feed your spirit richly. Each of these paths has strong advantages and disadvantages. Volunteer situations often carry considerable freedom to experiment. Because it lacks the perceived high stakes of a paid position, volunteer status allows you some room to try on new personalities and styles and to test out new skills in a relatively safe environment.

In fact, there are fields in which it is difficult to be hired without significant volunteer experience. Fair or not, there are reasons why this is true.

- In the arts, you simply have to cultivate and free up your talent before you're employable.
- In many service fields, such as human rights and crisis counseling, many people come in through a volunteer path; that is because there is no short-cut for the experience necessary to tap into the inner resources that make you effective. This path lets candidates show potential employers (and themselves) that they can not only perform but cope.
- In many startups, whether of businesses or non-profit organizations, months if not years of time can be invested in defining, testing and articulating a concept in a way that will attract financial backing.
- Similarly, researchers often invest unpaid time in developing proposals for funding. And even the most experienced journalists may reluctantly spend some time putting together article proposals on speculation.

Be warned: in some of these situations, the fields are structured in ways that quite unfairly demand freebies from the novice practitioner. Still, the challenge of breaking in remains — without feeding these trends and without letting oneself be exploited.

Jonathan Hickman graduated from Vassar College with a degree in English, a passion for video and a history of environmental activism that he never saw as a possible career. Hickman worked for a year in a publishing job that was a poor fit, then — to regroup — worked as a temp. He was assigned to the prestigious Council on Economic Priorities in New York City, an early leadership organization for corporate social responsibility. Not since Vassar had Hickman felt so close to heaven. When the temp job ended, he proposed a part-time volunteer position that would facilitate a professional courtship. He wrote research reports on the environmental performance of large corporations — while continuing to temp elsewhere for dollars. After "only" a year, he ended up with a full-time job that's the envy of many: as a researcher on a major project to document the best companies for ethnic minorities to work in. Two years out of college, his work was published by *Fortune* magazine.

Depending on the organization where you choose to volunteer, you may or may not receive quality supervision and leadership. Similarly, you may or may not be regarded as an equal member of the team. In many organizations, it is up to the volunteer to define the relationship, not to mention setting limits on it. Finally, it is always important to examine the consequences of volunteering in an organization where one wants to work for income in the future. Depending on the circumstances, the volunteer experience could be seen as a strong plus, or it could lead you to be identified as "different" from the paid staff.

In many business settings, the entrepreneurial approach gives you higher status and credibility than volunteering. In many non-profit settings, the reverse is true. But these boundaries are blurring rapidly. Businesses are realizing the feats accomplished by low-resourced, high-stakes non-profit work. Many non-profits are eager to attract entrepreneurial juice.

You can learn a lot, and fast, by dealing with the practical questions an entrepreneur must face: how to price a service or product and how to market it in a systematic fashion. However, you can also get sidetracked into building a business for its own sake, to the detriment of your original goals.

Support and commitment go hand in hand. Commitment in isolation may be unthinkable; commitment in community doesn't guarantee success, but allows an idea to bear whatever fruits it contains and allows the idea-holder to move through the development process with some grace.

The way this works is highly individualized. But a typical example is the life-changing experience of David Griswold, who worked in the office of an innovative non-profit called Ashoka, which matches social innovators with financial and strategic supporters around the world. When his wife got a year's job in Mexico, Griswold talked his way into accompanying Ashoka Fellow Arturo Garcia to work in Mexico's coffee country. "I thought I might pick coffee or something," he recalls. "But soon the coffee farmers — who were organized into small cooperatives — started opening up to us and saying, 'What we really need is some help in marketing our crops in the US.'" Griswold and Garcia made an initial foray, visiting nearly a hundred coffee wholesalers and being rejected by them all.

Amid the rejections, though, were seeds of future projects. A visit to Ben & Jerry's led eventually to a coffee ice cream partnership. The pair's first success, however, came when they knocked on the door of Paul Katzeff's northern California business, Thanksgiving Coffees. "Not just a cup, but a just cup" is the slogan of Katzeff's mail-order business, fueled by the former social worker and job trainer's visits to Nicaragua in the mid-1980s. Thanksgiving is committed to buying from farming cooperatives and to supporting organic farming methods, in the interest of safety for both consumers and workers.

Griswold and Garcia formed Aztec Coffees, a two-person shop in the US that buys the top-of-the-line beans from nine Mexican cooperatives, supporting some 15,000 farmers. These are sold to Ben & Jerry's for a new flavor, Aztec Coffee; and to Thanksgiving for its new Aztec Harvest blend. So serious were they about empowering the coffee growers that they issued stock to the cooperative owners and made themselves salaried employees. At times in the first few years, even those salaries were deferred.

For Griswold, the gamble was manageable because his family — with Peace Corps and Presbyterian missionary ties — backed him from the start. But he has been drawn into a much deeper commitment than he ever expected from his original Mexican jaunt. He reflects,

> I thought I would set up this little business and then move on, maybe go to law school or business school. But in the process, I developed a relationship with a lot of people in Mexico who had stuck their necks out to work with us. One collaborator in Oaxaca, Arturo Zavaleta, drew me aside once during a very difficult period. He said, "Down here, in the rainy season, when the rivers swell, the campesinos know that you can't turn back if the water is too rough. You have to keep going and get across." He drove home the point that there were a lot of people down there counting on me. Every time I would feel ready to bag it and go to business school, they would take me by the lapels and say, "Hold on, gringo."

Griswold's commitment, in turn, has made him able to attract other high-powered resources at very little cost. "I have friends who are consultants, lawyers, graphic designers and so on who have a great interest in what I'm doing. And they're always willing to pitch in, whether it's to design a logo or stay up late to ponder problems."

Most of us have been damaged, in one way or another, with respect to commitment. We have been pushed beyond our safety zone by well-meaning parents, teachers and friends. We have been given too much space or protection, too little structure. We have been challenged unkindly. Many of our role models of commitment are actually living wildly out-of-balance lives, like athletes on steroids. No wonder it is hard to commit ourselves in a way that is focused and self-respecting. As you explore the specific commitments that you are ready to make, it is useful to spend some time reflecting, and even journaling, on ways that your stance toward commitment may be a little off balance. For example:

- What positive memories do you associate with commitment and self-discipline?
- What negative memories? You might do some journal writing on each set of memories.
- What commitments, related to your working life directly or to your personal development, have you had trouble with?
- What specifically gets in the way?
- How would your life change if you were able to keep any one of these commitments?
- Is there anything scary about moving into that new life?
- What barriers to these commitments could you set about dismantling?
- What kinds of help would you need to do that and where might you find it?

The bravest aspect of a commitment is often the initial decision to let it into your life. After you say yes, opportunities for action have a way of presenting themselves. Rob Yeager, a record producer who spent 20 years too busy with other people's music to write his own, felt a stronger and stronger desire to express himself through music. But his responsibilities to his job and three children did not vanish. For months, Rob was too overwhelmed to take any action, except in a moment of inspiration, to move his three guitars out of storage and arrange them in his office. Committing himself only to face them every day, he soon responded to their silent presence. Rob began to write songs.

Stepping into *Your* Commitment

These are some thoughts about commitment in general. Now — back to you. You are about to create something. Its elements are entirely in the realm of ideas and experience — but they are powerful. What you create, starting now, will move you into action on your vision somehow. What you are about to create is a set of simple commitments based upon the answers to three questions:

- What's the work to be done that expresses your essence in today's specific context — what do you want to achieve, what choices of occupation and industry let you do it?

- Who can you collaborate with to take some constructive action without waiting for a job or business to gel?
- What simple things can you do, starting now, to enact your commitment to the work and visibly advance it?

If you find yourself reacting to some of the possibilities by obsessing on the possible downside, you're not alone. The following exercise helps put the risks of any contemplated change into perspective by considering also the benefits of making the change — and the risks and benefits of staying put. A simple grid helps you organize these four elements and then look at them all together.

This can be copied and used to explore any number of risks that you might be faced with. For each, identify the risks of jumping in, the risks of hanging back, the benefits of each — and then consider how you can manage or sidestep the risks and maximize the benefits.

Make a list of all the activities that could be part of doing your work without waiting to be paid. Consider options from all the categories in the Life/Work Wheel you used in Step 2 to envision how you want your life to be, realizing that commitments outside the specific world of work can open your vocational options up — from socializing to working out to spending time in nature to enhance your creativity. In each category, write down specific actions you could take to advance your work without waiting to be paid. A few examples on the worksheet show how this exercise can open up unexpected options.

In this list of potential commitments, include ideas that are big and small, wild and cautious. Identify the ones that are possible in light of your current situation. Now, among those possible actions, identify the ones that seem to have the most potential for moving you along in a sustainable fashion. Do any of these seem exciting? Choose items from this short list, one at a time and consider what might happen if you took this action. Hang onto the possible actions that have the most "life" in your imagination and discard the rest. Sort these options:

Volunteer actions   Entrepreneurial actions

_____

_____

_____

_____

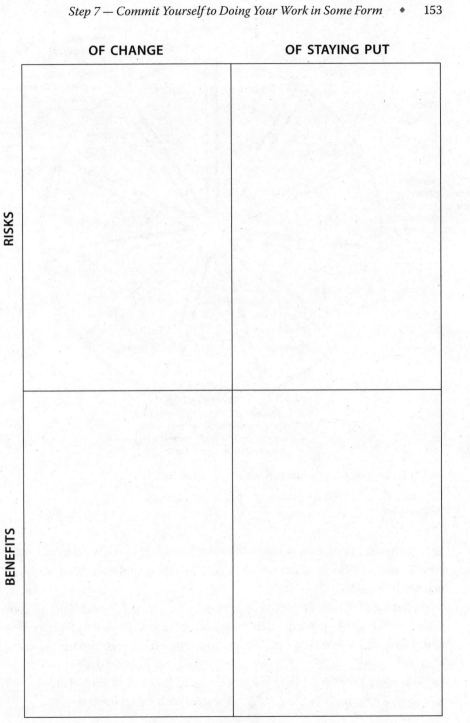

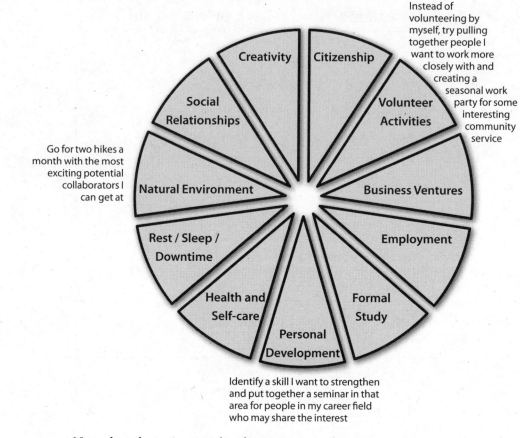

Instead of volunteering by myself, try pulling together people I want to work more closely with and creating a seasonal work party for some interesting community service

Go for two hikes a month with the most exciting potential collaborators I can get at

Identify a skill I want to strengthen and put together a seminar in that area for people in my career field who may share the interest

Now place the actions you've chosen on a timeline.

Today	This week	This month	Next month

What's missing to turn these steps into a clear path that could plausibly bring your work to fruition and strengthen your contacts with the world of work you want to be paid in?

What kinds of support would be necessary for you to follow this path? Consider financing, workspace, equipment, complementary skills you may lack and, above all, social support. Where and how could you line up these resources?

This assessment brings us back, full circle, to the explorations of Steps 1 and 2. And so we replay here the Life/Work Wheel with a final invitation:

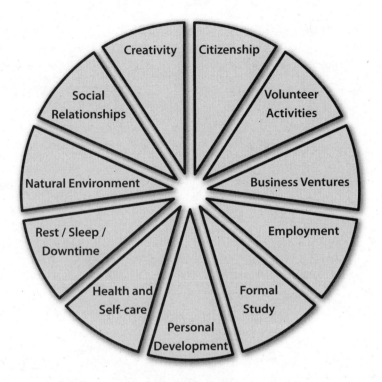

Scan the categories of life represented on the wheel, from employment and business opportunities to citizenship and time in nature. How can they work together? Consider hikes with potential business associates; citizen actions that use your writing skill to publish letters to the editor that will go into your portfolio; deep discussion with family and close friends about how to strengthen your network in community; consulting on an aspect of your work that you would like to build into a business or be hired to do. How can these elements, organized as a coherent whole, help you create a working life that will ultimately pay the bills, provide meaning and make an impact?

Finally, then, what is it that you will make a personal commitment to — your work and the ways you will do it as you move into action mode?

Plan and Organize Your Campaign

Sentiment without action is the ruin of the soul.

Edward Abbey

Creating the working life you love, is work in itself. But it doesn't have to be a grim assault on the mountain peak — and in fact, it works better if it's approached much more lightly. What you are looking to do is orchestrate a move, into the position that best fits you, with the help of a support system that you have been systematically creating through the earlier steps in this book. This chapter walks you through the job search process, from the "strength perspective" we have developed.

If you are awake, you are well focused on the arenas of greatest interest and able to make focused use of the resources around you.

If your life is relatively stabilized, you will have enough time, money and inner resources, and you will be decently organized — an excellent qualification for a job or investment candidate in its own right.

If you have created a vibrant support system, then your key people know what to do and will reliably do it. You are not alone.

If you are clear about the landscape, your strengths and the essence of your work, then you will be able to step confidently forward.

If you have begun to live a life of commitment to that work — separately from your employment status, finding ways to have an impact and a life — then you should be working *with* the dynamics of your industry, occupational field and community of concern. You should be aware of the work being done around you, the funding streams, the ebb and flow of organizations and the range of opportunities.

This makes it much, much easier to develop an organized job search or business startup. We will focus here on the job search, but many of the principles are transferable to starting a business.

Setting Your Sights

In Step 4, we reviewed ways to prospect for published and hidden job leads by:
- Reviewing the job listings in general and specialty publications for your industry/professional/trade association and arena of interest
- Reviewing the publications, blogs, websites and meeting agendas for your arena of interest to see where there is investment and activity
- Asking your network of informants where the hiring is in those specific areas, and in the field generally, and where hiring is expected in the next three months.

If you are determined to make a job change in a fairly short period of time, I recommend challenging yourself to generate a slightly inflated list of at least 6 to 10 good leads at a time. In a specialized field, this is hard to do. Some of them will be right on target, but others may be good jobs that use your core skills but may be less directly on your path of the heart. Or they will involve compromises of geography or compensation. Choose from your list of options, the 3 to 6 that you will apply for right now, thus reviewing which criteria are flexible in your mind right now and which aren't. Then focus your creativity on carrying out a superb application process for each one.

Please, please make a file for each potential employer and take a little time to keep notes on conversations, correspondence and so on. See the worksheet below.

A superb application process means a customized one. This is easiest to do when you are dealing with people, rather than applying for positions online. While at times online applications are necessary, the strategy outlined here is based on minimizing them.

If human contact is possible, get in touch by phone with the contact person identified in the job ad or given to you by your informants. Being very businesslike and respectful of their time, ask whether there is a more detailed job description available and how you can obtain a copy. Usually these can be e-mailed, faxed or mailed to you. At the same time, inquire about the application deadline and the timeline for the decision after that. This will be useful later.

Communication Log

Employer name _____

Address _____

_____

Main phone _____

Contact person, phone, e-mail _____

_____

Hiring manager, phone, e-mail _____

_____

Website _____

Date _____

Activity _____

_____

Follow-up needed _____

Employer name _____

Address _____

_____

Main phone _____

Contact person, phone, e-mail _____

_____

Hiring manager, phone, e-mail _____

_____

Website _____

Date _____

Activity _____

_____

Follow-up needed _____

Looking beyond the job description to the real significance of the job, your direct informants will help — as much as they are ethically able. Use the help while respecting their boundaries. For example, before asking them questions, it helps to clarify: "If you're comfortable sharing this info..." Your goal is to learn about the hiring process — the organization's most important needs, reasons why the position is open now, what the organization might be wary about, reasons other people didn't work out in the position, pressures on the hire from inside or outside the organization, who is most influential in the decision. You want to know what it will take to get hired, but you don't want to send the signal that you are trying to go around due process or obtain unfair advantage. Instead of asking "How do I get hired at _____?", therefore, ask, "How do I make sure my application gets full and fair attention?"

Telling Your Story

If your targeting is fairly clear and your self-assessment has been thorough, there is a payoff right now: developing your marketing materials will be simpler than you may have thought. It's time to create (or polish) your:

- Résumé
- Standard cover letter (which will of course be customized)
- List of references
- Personal portfolio — the examples of your work that can be brought together in almost any field

Your résumé is a legal document, as well as a marketing piece. This is a little like the fact that light is both a wave and a particle. A legal document must be accurate, thorough and reasonably neutral. A marketing piece must also be accurate, but it is much more selective and is expected to have a point of view. Some guidelines for balancing these requirements:

- Never lie and never willfully mislead.
- Make sure that the major themes and periods of your career are covered, while focusing in the most detail on those themes that are relevant to the current search.
- Include your major responsibilities and accomplishments showing the highest possible level of skill, but do not entirely omit major responsibilities you had, at which your performance was less dazzling.

- While it is fine to adapt aspects of your résumé for particular positions (such as the objective and professional summary), remember that copies of your résumé may be forwarded to others without your knowledge, and that two (different) copies could end up on the same person's desk (for example, if you are applying for several positions in the same institution or occupational specialty and the hiring managers know each other).

Résumé formats and strategies are well documented by a number of coaches and authors. My favorite is Yana Parker's *Damn Good Résumé Guide* (damn good.com). Her examples, and tips on how to handle résumé challenges, are recommended.

To recall and organize the material that will go into your résumé, you might begin with a review of your major accomplishments at work or in related areas such as school or volunteer activity. Consider both the things you were formally recognized for and those you were simply proud of. Ordinary work counts. Refer back to the Accomplishments Worksheet in Step 5. You can review the skills that you used and make sure these are stated clearly to match the skills identified in the job announcement.

The most important aspects of the résumé are the ones that bring you alive as a candidate and make your fit for a particular situation very clear. The places to focus your creative résumé work are the professional summary and your statement of objective — two opening sections that can each be read in less than a minute and can, if well crafted, keep the reader intrigued.

The **summary** ties together *who you are* as a working person: your core skills and the way you have used them. It can draw attention to your seniority, your unusual achievements, the way you go at your work, what makes you stand out.

The **objective statement** tells where you want to go now — and may be customized for particular kinds of positions. It should be broader than the specific job you are applying for, but encompass it.

In detailing out your career history, just a few principles are key:

- Be as concise as possible.
- Visually structure it for readability.
- Focus on your achievements and impacts, not just roles and responsibilities.

Even if the voice is fairly neutral, the achievements and impacts that you choose to highlight will say a good bit about your values and the kind of employee you are. For example, a senior economic and business development official in county government, with corporate management background, included in his bulleted list of turnaround management accomplishments, "Restructured $38 million company and retooled manufacturing operation without losing a single employee" — an achievement that not every manager would think relevant to highlight.

Extra flourishes — personal and family data, outside interests — are optional. If you include them, be very concise. Family information may tip off an employer to talk with you about schools or relocation support. Mentioning interests shows that you have a life — but overemphasis will look self-indulgent. Keep this to two or three lines at most.

It is not necessary to note that references are available. In fact, you should include a one-page typed sheet of them, with full contact information and a line or two about the relationship of each reference to you so that potential employers can target their questions effectively.

Cover Letter

Contrary to popular literature, your goal is not to "knock 'em dead." Your goal is to engage the people you want to work for and with, clearly and professionally, and to help them see your value in a way that will be borne out when you are actually in the position. Hype backfires.

This does not mean you should be bland. There are a number of good ways to ensure that your letter will be read and remembered. Specifics and details are remembered, especially when they are one-of-a-kind. For example:

- Include a few lines about an experience that drew you into the work you are doing and why you have sustained that commitment. "As my résumé shows, I have worked in industrial toxics reduction for over 15 years. While the early years were challenging as we educated co-workers about the reasons our positions existed, I've grown with the field because I have developed some leading programs to do that education effectively."
- Tell a *brief, sharp* story about how you have handled a challenge similar to those you expect in the new job. "In addition to serving clients in a standard health center setting, I've had a chance to go into communities in a mobile testing unit and talk with young people about health and lifestyle choices. In fact, I would like to discuss with you whether some of your programs

might take advantage of the County's resources to reach into communities this way."

- Mention any connection you may have to the area where the workplace is located. "I've passed your offices on the way to my daughter's soccer practice for years, so it will be very rewarding to meet you and perhaps be there on a regular basis."

A warm yet professional cover letter that shows who you are along with what you do will leave the kind of impression that gets you the interview. And that is the purpose of the cover letter:

- It clearly shows that you fit or exceed the specific requirements of the job.
- It goes on to show your comparative advantage — what you bring that other candidates may not.
- It brings you to life as a person that others would like to work with.
- It gets you selected for one or more interviews, at which the sale can be closed.

I mentioned a portfolio that illustrates your work. This is well understood by artists, writers, architects and graphic designers. But everybody does stuff, and some of it is yours to show off. A photograph of a cabinet you have built or a stream you have helped to restore, a sample grant proposal that you have gotten funded or media coverage of an event that you have produced all help to reinforce your message of skill and productivity.

Your references should be developed at the beginning of a search and used as consistently as possible. Call anyone you will be asking for a professional reference and make sure they remain comfortable doing this, even if they have served as your references in the past. Ask whether their memory of your work is clear and, if not, e-mail them your updated résumé as a refresher, with a brief note of thanks. Whenever you are about to apply for a position where a particular reference will be key, let them know in an e-mail that they should expect a call and mention any highlights of the position that would help them to address your most relevant strengths.

Opening the Door

"Don't just apply for a job. Campaign for it," advises Seattle career counselor Pres Winslow. This does not mean cheerleading or shallow self-promotion. It means orchestrating a sustained effort to demonstrate your qualifications, maintain your visibility, understand any barriers to hiring you and help to dissolve them if you can.

The first step is getting your application into play. In putting the application together, follow directions (even if it hurts). If multiple copies are requested, or if there's a "no phone calls please" line at the bottom or if there is a request for salary history, honor these requests — skillfully. For example:

- No phone calls from you doesn't mean no phone calls from a mutual colleague who can check on the status of your application.
- If you are asked to identify, up front, the compensation you are looking for, identify a well-researched range and qualify that this is "based on my current understanding of the scope of responsibility."
- If you are asked to include salary history, do this only if there is evidence that your application will not be read without it; in this case, identify a range and add that your requirements for the current position are dependent on its responsibilities, not on history.

Interviews

I know a few people who get themselves a job interview every year or two, whether they need it or not. It's about keeping in practice. But they also enjoy the experience.

In a competitive win/lose world, a job interview is the quintessential verbal combat, an opportunity to be judged and to reveal (or hide) your shortcomings. In a win/win context, a job interview is a dialogue to uncover your fit for a particular opportunity and how to make things work in an organization. You, as a job candidate, are actually a resource to the employer by showing your understanding of how the work is done, the qualifications most needed, the trade-offs and the way the position should grow with the organization.

I realized this fully, during a stint as executive director of a non-profit scientific research institute, when we needed to hire a technical specialist far outside our own expertise. It was at the beginning of the West Nile Virus scare about five years ago, and we had been awarded a County health department contract to monitor the wetlands where the offending mosquitoes might breed. We needed to hire a tropical medicine specialist — in upstate New York. We spent many weeks flying in candidates from more tropical areas and were both impressed and grateful to see how the best ones carefully educated us about the nuances of skill needed to do their jobs. Several advised us on the project budgeting, the kinds of support staff we would need and potential communication issues with our clients. One — who decided not to leave his home base — even sent us a list of other candidates to consider interviewing!

Most working people understand the homework required to prepare for an interview. It does not need to be lengthy, but does need to include:

- Updating your background research on the employer and being on top of any recent news coverage or changes
- Preparing some informed questions to ask and an icebreaker line or two for the opening moments
- Gathering any background information you can on the specific people you will be meeting with (whose names and positions you can generally learn by asking who they are, when you are invited to interview)
- Bringing extra copies of your résumé and supporting documents for everyone, just in case
- A drive-by or Mapquest to be clear on location and travel time.

Note that there are limits to the questions that can legally be asked in an employment interview in the United States. Questions that could serve as a basis for discrimination — about your spiritual life or religion, your ethnic or cultural background, sexual orientation, age or handicapping conditions — are off limits. Questions about your ability to do the job are not. This matters especially if you are not hired and believe that discrimination may have taken place. What to do with an illegal question depends on the context. If the question is asked in a way that reveals unsavory attitude on the employer's part, there might be a red flag with respect to the job. However, one interviewer's misstep should not deprive you of an opportunity in a basically healthy and well-run organization. If the question appears to be without malice, one strategy is to reply with an answer to a related question that would be legal, acting as though the interviewer hadn't crossed the line. That is, if you're asked your age, say "Old enough to have seen how this industry has evolved and young enough to have quite a bit of time left — thank goodness!" A New Agey but wonderful employer once asked me, in a hiring interview, the illegal question "What is your spiritual path?" Feeling a boundary violated, I responded, "Deep and personal." I was hired.

Back to the substance of the interview process and its chemistry. While details will vary, the conversation will begin by exploring your specific qualifications in terms of skills and experience; it will then move into discussion of your specific strengths and shortcomings. Tours and opportunities to meet other employees may be signs of progress, or additional opportunities to check you out.

If these phases go well enough, then a hiring discussion will begin — often with additional players at the table. It speaks well of a potential employer when there is thoughtful discussion of how you will work with specific other people, how you intend to approach the work, how potential difficulties may be handled. One very strong arts administrator, applying for a leadership job in a troubled symphony orchestra, used the hiring interview as a venue for discussing some limitations of her experience, such as lack of financial crisis management experience.

Below is a list of commonly used interview questions along with some keys to effective responses. Understand the reasons behind them and the information they generate, and prepare your thoughts (if not your words). If you are well prepared for these, you will probably handle any others just fine.

1. *Tell me about yourself.*
   Set the agenda, define your fit for the position, show preparation and clear communication

2. *Why do you think you fit with this position?*
   State or restate your relevant skills at the highest level you've exercised them and show you understand what's really important in the position.

3. *What can you bring that other candidates might not?*
   Show your distinctive strengths without ever belittling other people.

4. *Why do you want to work for us?*
   Show your appreciation of challenge, your values as they mesh with the organization's and your knowledge of what they're about.

5. *What do you know about us?*
   Show the homework you have done, show empathy, avoid flattery.

6. *Why are you in the job market right now?*
   Whatever is going on, be matter-of-fact and enthusiastic.

7. *Tell me about a challenge you have faced in your last position and how you handled it.*
Show responsibility and initiative, show you understand the complexity of problems and demonstrate your inventiveness in getting to a solution.

8. *What kind of compensation are you looking for?*
Give them a well-researched range of no more than $20,000 based on your knowledge of what similar jobs pay; qualify that this is "based on my current understanding of the scope of responsibility."

9. *What kinds of work environments are you most at home and effective in?*
Be honest and suggest ways you would handle any rough aspects of the fit between your ideal and this job.

10. *How has your education prepared you for this position?*
Focus on kinds of learning experiences, networks and mentors that are uniquely yours and strengthen your suit, not just degrees.

11. *Where do you see yourself going in the next five years?*
Outline a plausible path that keeps you in the organization for 3 to 5 years and focus on your contribution there.

12. *How would you handle _____ [specific job challenge]?*
Say what's clear and include how you would find guidance if you don't know the answer.

13. *What is the stupidest thing you have done in your career?*
We all have them. Pick a light one.

14. *Do you have any questions for us right now?*
Oh, yes. Ask questions that show your knowledge, understanding of the work and (hopefully authentic) pleasure in getting to know these people.

A common interview dilemma is whether — and how — to raise tough questions or express doubts. One non-profit executive I know chose to push the conversation at the hiring interview into her areas of limited experience. This was to be sure the hiring team was making a realistic, wholehearted decision. And it also demonstrated her professionalism and authenticity very well.

If you are a good fit for the job and exploring whether you're the best fit, honest candor can work in your favor. Joanie, an educational psychologist applying for a high-powered job in a school system, got completely disoriented in her home city on the way to the interview. She knew where she was going but drifted into that peculiar brain-fog that takes over in the presence of strong emotions. She knew it was a sign of her mixed feelings about the job. On arrival, she put on the Interview Mask and impressed the superintendent's staff with her qualifications. But something about the conversation just felt too unreal. She blurted at the end:

> I want to discuss one other thing. On the way here, I had some really strong feelings about whether or not I'm a fit for this job, and they were so overpowering that I drove in circles. And I was embarrassed to tell you that. But I can't walk out of here pretending I want to work for people I don't feel safe enough with to share something like that. And I like you, so I'm opening my mouth.

The interviewers laughed, prolonged the conversation for another half hour to discuss the ways the school system had been struggling with staff communication issues and hired Joanie because they thought her directness and bravery might help the situation.

The rituals that formalize working relationships — from interviews to performance reviews to company outings — are exquisite reflections about what a society really believes. So it fits that norms of interviewing and hiring are in tremendous flux. On one end of a spectrum, there is the increasing use of psychological testing, group interviews, computerized scanning of résumés and other tools that aim to support more rigorous decision-making (at lower cost). There is at least one approach to getting clear, or clearer, about measuring what matters. At the other extreme, there are stories about interviews in which the conversation jumped out of the box — as if interviewer and candidate forged a non-verbal agreement to test out each other's risk levels — and people got hired explicitly for the virtues of self-knowledge, self-respect and communication skill.

At the very least, this means the game is not as narrow as the rulebook, and the interview is an opportunity to test what's possible in doing the actual work.

Whether you are a job-seeker or potential contractor exploring a match, or a person with an idea doing the mating dance with financial backers, remember that an interview isn't just where you try to get a yes. It's where you try to get a yes that doesn't launch a disastrous mismatch — for example, by discussing your honest hopes, strengths and struggles concretely with your manager-to-be; by looking at how tough dilemmas have been handled and letting your readings on organizational integrity inform your decision about whether to take the job.

After the interview, if you are functioning in true campaign mode, you may even have a set of thank-you cards and stamps in your briefcase. Right after the interview, try to have time to sit down for a coffee, make notes on things you have learned and any miscommunications to correct and, at the same time, write up a simple, clear thank-you note and get it into the mail. If you sense that your message didn't come across too strongly, it is permissible to write a follow-up letter that opens with a phrase like "On further reflection." This kind of a letter can also be used to remind the potential employer of your talents as the interviewing period nears its close — the reason I encouraged you at the beginning to try hard to get that information.

A job search involves a good measure of tasks we would rather not be doing, from typing to snooping. Keeping it organized keeps it on track and maintains confidence. Be sure to organize complementary activities that remind you of your humanity and intrinsic value separate from the search — from helping out at the local food bank to climbing the local mountain. Structure in the search is a form of spiritual practice. It does not necessarily imply that we think all our focus and attention to detail will in fact get us the job. But they create conditions that will bring good things to life.

Plan (and Prepare) to Work
with the Unknown

Dr. Martin Luther King did not say "I have a strategic plan."

Eric Britton

The anarchy of these times has at least one positive consequence. New ideas are being adopted, and new rules written, by thousands of people without conventional status or successful track records. Originality has never been more of an advantage. Shift your line of sight even one degree away from the obvious, and you will almost certainly notice unexpected possibilities for new careers, clientele, styles of working and ways to contribute.

But wait. You have made a plan and created the tools to support the plan's success. Yes. Just don't take any of that too seriously. The opportunities will come when you simultaneously plan and know when to throw away the plan.

Denise Caywood, a newly certified massage therapist, was running dry in her job hunt until she had a dream about trucks and set up a muscular therapy practice in the Triple-T Truck Stop outside Tucson.

Jim Malloy, a business professor at Northeastern University, designed a popular course in business development, specifically for athletes on the major sports teams who are getting ready to retire.

These stories show the power of approaching your work as an infinite game. No finite attitude, no matter how generous or how right it may be in some circumstances, is adequate to deal with the degree of flux and complexity out there. What's more, no finite attitude can match the complexity in you and open you up to the inner resources you need in order to respond to the shifting context. Planning is essential. But that doesn't mean it's enough.

These times call for four particular kinds of assumption-busting:

1. Don't assume that the organizations, sectors and job fields that have been your home in the past will continue to be hospitable.
2. Don't assume that the organizations, sectors and fields you have ruled out in the past will continue to be off limits.
3. Don't assume that the outward manifestations of a job — the forms and formalities — are a major indicator of security or satisfaction. There is much more going on, and some of it is positive.
4. Don't assume that there's a single right next step or even a single right path for you. You get to choose.

Assumption-busting helps us to be attentive to the opportunities that are right here, right now. Jane, a social worker, realized this a few months after she was laid off. She spent part of every week playing the role of an unemployed person: collecting her check, answering job ads, having weighty conversations about the future. Another part of her life was devoted to activities she loved: a small private practice and a satisfying volunteer role in her community, producing cultural activities such as cabarets and storytelling festivals. But the enjoyment didn't feel right. "I have to stop all these free-floating projects and figure out my career!" a voice in her mind kept screaming. Then, in a workshop, she had an opportunity to list her strengths and skills and examine the possibilities they presented. Scanning them, she realized: "These projects aren't a distraction from my work. They are my work! I can make a living by marketing these ideas."

To be anchored in a sense of personal purpose and a community of shared values is a necessary replacement for other kinds of anchors that are no longer reliable, such as structured career paths, generous organizations and reliable information about where security lies. Nobody really knows whether this will be enough. Nobody really knows the impact on coherent decision-making and planning of the climate of constant flux in which so many people live and work. But it is clear that the art form of this era is living with a combination of clear identity and flexible strategy.

That combination is illustrated in the career of Gay Canough, a PhD physicist who now makes her living installing solar energy systems. Canough admits that her career had its roots in *Star Trek*. She was always fascinated by outer space and drawn to seek human benefits through exploration, such as mining asteroids for metals. She started a company called ExtraTerrestrial Materials, developed technology concepts and saw some implemented. But she found that the needs for funding and institutional support for deep-space initiatives did not exactly favor the small entrepreneur. She became involved in the design of a successful probe that was built and launched to seek water on the moon. She got involved in space solar power and became a world expert on the science of beaming the energy back to Earth using wireless transmission. At a conference, she spoke with a colleague who was installing a solar energy system just a few miles from her home. She says:

> This is the point where my brain switched to terrestrial solar power. He asked, "If you are going to do space solar power, shouldn't you do terrestrial solar power first?" This little light bulb went off. I had been looking for some resource in space that I could make money on without actually dealing with space travel. So I'm walking around with the sun beating on my head and thought AHA! A space resource that I don't have to go to space to find! I did a study for NASA to consider when we needed the big space power stations versus generation on Earth. What I discovered was that you don't need the space solar power plant unless you are trying to get all your power from the sun in New York City, a tall skinny city without enough rooftop space.

From this epiphany came ETM SolarWorks, her successful installation company.

Whatever may bring you these breakthroughs, they probably won't come from trying too hard. Virginia Kellogg now has a successful practice as a personal coach, based in rural Pennsylvania and working with clients around the world to help them achieve their goals, and she reflects:

> About four years ago, I was pretty lost. I had been teaching my kids, doing lots of outside work on leading personal empowerment workshops and just knew some change was needed. I did not have a clue. I spent a year working hard to figure out the best thing to do, exploring possibilities and still I was no closer to an answer.
>
> One day I was sitting by the pond writing. This is something I do lots, and I have been for years open to the messages that the natural world sends my way. This day the pines on the hillsides just seemed to be telling me to "ask and listen and act." So I did. I simply told whatever the power is that listens (spirit) that I needed to be told what to do. That I

would commit to do whatever it was, no second-guessing, no asking questions. I knew this commitment to myself and spirit was crucial. I totally accepted whatever came my way and committed to DO IT.

My whole being relaxed. I knew that this was right. It was several days later, while walking down the road, that I felt literally "hit in the face" with a thought that I needed to help people pull their lives together, in balance. I had no clue how to do this but I dove in that day. Immediately doors opened (money, training, clarification of the path), and it has not stopped.

What made the difference was daring to notice that the answers were speaking to me all around me. Someone told me later: "The intuitive mind will instruct the thinking mind where to look next."

That open, "assumptionless" state of mind can be supported by a slowdown, when possible. John Cleese, formerly a *Monty Python* comic, has achieved success in a new career, using high-voltage humor in the workplace through his corporate training company. He made the move by "taking some tortoise time." During the transition, Cleese told the *New York Times*,

> The truth is, I don't know where I go now. If you try to plan with your hare brain, you'll think along the lines of what you've done before. The only way that you find a slightly new direction at this kind of juncture is to create a space and see what flows into it.[1]

On one level, the decision-making that shapes a life's work can be reduced to a series of resolutions to dilemmas:

- Shall I work as an employee or entrepreneur right now?
- Shall I take this weekend workshop or go to the mountains?
- Shall I gamble on my future in this organization by committing to another extra project, or update my résumé and spend my free time networking?
- Shall I stick my neck out on these administrative battles now, or save my energy for the environmental initiative we're planning next month?

Behind every either-or decision, there is a less polarized way of asking what's real and important about values, needs, priorities and strategies. While rising to the daily dilemmas, we are challenged to go deeper and find a synthesis that lets us be increasingly clear on our core values and increasingly true to them.

All this requires a flexibility of response and a deeper flexibility of mind, anchored by a set of core values and loyalties that are continuously clarified. You can't fathom the resources that will come into your life. You can't predict the time frame for change. You can't guess the kindred spirits you'll meet, or the complementary organizations and projects you'll bump into at conferences or even in the course of doing your work. You can only keep on carrying the ball, using your best skills and pay attention to changes around you — including those that result from your actions. But doing "only" this can have a near-miraculous impact on learning and creativity. Here's Natalie Goldberg again, discussing the way discipline and openness intersect in meditation or any other practice (such as the practice of lifelong clarification of one's work):

> I've watched meditation students come and go. They use anything as an excuse — "My knee hurt," "The teacher said *he* instead of *she!*" "The schedule just wasn't good for me." There is no excuse: If you want it, go for it. Don't let anything toss you away. The other extreme is to accept blindly everything a teacher does: He's sleeping indiscriminately with the women in the community and you think, "Well, it's part of the teachings." It is best to stay alive, alert, trust yourself, but not give up, no matter what the situation. Get in there, stay in there, figure it out. If we want the teachings, we have to let ourselves be hungry. If a green pepper is offered, eat it. If it's a steak, devour it. If it's something indigestible — a turd, a cement block, a shoe — figure out what to do with it but don't back away.

This kind of flexibility is not a passive or indecisive stance. It's about showing up and "waiting for instructions" in a very alert, disciplined, responsive and playful spirit — paying attention to the subtleties of every decision, doing your best to be well prepared to respond to the right opportunities and even taking initiative to test out the wrong ones. It means treating each situation as unique and making the fullest possible use of all the faculties you have developed in response to it.

That is, use all you have and give all you can, without depleting yourself in a way that makes it impossible to bounce back. When you have fewer assumptions to fall back on as a source of structure, the arts of limit-setting and dynamic decision-making become much more crucial to living through times of uncertainty. Saying yes and no appropriately are both acts of self-affirmation.

Hyper-adventurousness — trying new things in a way that's out of proportion with your ability to assimilate them — is just as damaging as hyper-protectiveness. To get a fix on whether I'm being open to a given opportunity in a spirit of relaxed faith or of compulsiveness, I rely on a handful of questions:

1. Am I looking at my options from the standpoint of what's needed, right now, to meet my goals or to address a specific problem — or am I driven by old business such as proving something to someone?

2. If I don't do this, will it be picked up by somebody else who is in a better position to accomplish it in a sustainable and healthy way? If nobody takes the action in question, will harm result?

3. Is there a simpler, less risky or labor-intensive means to the same end?

Part of healthy limit-setting is realizing that all you have to give will not be enough to bring to life the great visions you're capable of seeing. Not enough by itself, that is. But tiny, isolated acts of unpredictable significance can often be a key element in helping major changes to take place. Think of the campaigns that have been won and lost by a handful of votes, and the number of businesses that have stayed open or folded based on the choices of a handful of customers or a critical investor. As Gandhi captured the paradox, "What you can do may be too small to matter, but it is very important that you do it."

Whenever you meet people who seem to understand this approach to work and life, ply them with pastries and get them to talking. It is these stories, rich and unpredictable, that provide the necessary models for letting go of self-imposed limits.

My first exposure to the art of assumptionless evolution was a meeting in Managua, Nicaragua, with a Seattle woman on her way to Alaska. I am going to tell you this story in some detail, because it runs counter to every form of "rational" career planning and yet has a logic which I believe is characteristic of a growing number of people's paths today.

In Central America for a conference, I happened to be sitting on the front porch of a small guest house when someone I'd interviewed years before pulled up to the curb. Not knowing I was in town, she was looking for a fellow guest I hadn't met yet. That is the coincidence that introduced me to Janet Levin, a teacher and writer with a "useless degree" in educational psychology.

Against the backdrop of a guerilla war, Levin was a shoestring traveler working with children, parents and teachers in communities touched by the war. Her project was simple but psychologically sophisticated: getting kids to draw pictures about their lives, and talking with parents and teachers about the meaning of those drawings for the children's development. Levin knew that, when people experience trauma, their ability to heal and reclaim their lives is increased a great deal if they are able to give some voice to their emotions soon after the fact. By helping adults to recognize and support the children's need for catharsis, she was also creating a structure for communities to find their voices.

Levin's leap of faith — "the kid pictures project" — resulted in a manuscript, *Guatemalan Guernica*; a traveling exhibition; media appearances and expressions of gratitude wherever she went. It led her on to demonstrate the same idea in a Russian village of resettled refugees from Chernobyl and in Alaskan fishing villages with high levels of domestic violence. Finally, Levin found her way into a tailor-made job in Alaska, directing a statewide counseling program to combat community violence. Here is how she tells the story:

> My work and life have been a spiral. Now that I'm 45, I can see from this vantage point how I've chosen each step. Each successive five-year period beginning with 20, I was involved with work and place I didn't know existed five years earlier. A five-year plan? I don't think so.
>
> It's taken years of groping in the darkness to realize that I actually had a system, even when I thought I was just groping. I often describe my process as "organic," which means that at times it stinks. I don't recommend my process to everyone.

She started out teaching kindergarten, and without trying to do anything unusual, she evolved an innovative open-classroom model good enough to attract the attention of the administration and be videotaped. That classroom contained the major elements that Levin would carry with her in the years to come: "comfort and curiosity in a culture not my own, children, families, community, poverty, innovation." And the tendency to take very thorough "breaks" from work every five years or so. Levin's first break was a trip southward, with Mexico as the carefully planned destination and Guatemala as the real end point.

> Traveling taught me to follow my feet. Yes, have a good map. Be knowledgeable about the surroundings, ask about safe places and restaurants. Talk to the locals and to the travelers. And then be still. Feel where you're drawn and move in that direction. When the street curves or

dead-ends, look around; pay attention; go toward your curiosity. Consistently a place or person of interest is there.

My experience in Guatemala affected my senses, but my mind didn't understand. That taught me the power of my own sensate experience. I didn't have to understand. My attention was firmly grabbed. I felt at home. At first, I thought it had to do with the geography and the Mayan culture. Now I'd say it's a state of being I learned.

Several aspects of Levin's lifestyle have made it much easier for her to follow her feet. She lives a life of material simplicity. When she is employed, she saves money fiercely. She barters, borrows and thrift-shops. And she has built a large network over the years that provides her with vigorous support. These are things that can expand anyone's flexibility; you only have to do them.

On her return, Levin had the predictable reverse culture shock and waves of insight about her place on the planet. She settled in the Pacific Northwest and took a series of jobs in early childhood education:

I mourned having to conform to a non-organic life. I couldn't follow my senses. I had to show up. But I didn't have to work full time, so half my awake time was passed strengthening "traveler's senses." I didn't really know what to do in this new situation, so the traveler in me went with the organic approach, and the evaluations were much like those in Philadelphia.

The ending of a grant coincided with a birthday visit to Eastern Oregon, an introduction at a party and by the end of the weekend, a job. A temporary one for five months that would leave me eligible to collect unemployment and my thoughts. I wanted out of the classroom. I wanted to work with terminally ill children. But it didn't happen on my timeline.

I spent five years as director of a university daycare co-op in Seattle, loving the people but not the work, all the while learning budget management and staff supervision. On my own time, I volunteered with the hospice, drawing with the kids and talking about their feelings. What was desire for change at 30 was a fever pitch by 35.

All the "organic" approach in the world did not get Levin off the hook for learning budget management and staff supervision, and being fully present to the left-brained aspects of her job. Nor does it take the place of planning and active prospecting for opportunities when it's time for a change. As Levin testifies:

> I have a Native drawing on my wall. It's a straight line, with a spiral, like DNA, going around it. The straight line stands for the planned actions I took to hunt for a job. I read the paper every day. I wrote letters, wonderful fictions, for jobs I didn't really want. I went to the employment service. I networked. As I was doing all these things, I had the distinct feeling that they were baby steps, but very necessary. Then there was another, simultaneous process: the spiral. It accounts for what I would call the outside influences: what's bigger than my ego or my perception. All the surprises. They're part of me, too, but they're bigger than my conscious mind could handle.

These two processes converged to lead Levin to Central America. She only knew she was deeply restless and suspected it would be a good idea to be in an unfamiliar place, "in order to pull the newness out of me."

> I thought, "Somebody should do a book of kid drawings in Central America, to let the kids speak for what's happening there." Then I met somebody who knew somebody who knew the bishop in southern Mexico, who was visiting in the US. I was introduced, and the bishop invited me to come and meet people who could get me into the refugee camps. All this I did. I ended up with 300 drawings and a changed life.

Can you think of any aspects of your career that have "always been this way" and seem unchangeable? How about industries, professions, trades or parts of the world you've always been in? Roles you've always played? Definitions of success that have always attracted you? Where and how did you decide that these were necessary? Is there anyone you're trying to please, or rebel against, by hanging onto these assumptions? When you have been in the most open, "assumptionless" states in your life, what conditions have helped you function that way? What has it been like to work, and make choices about work, in that state?

Try this. Go around and ask people you respect, whose work you find fascinating, how they ended up in their present jobs. You will find all kinds of non-linear stories. You may even notice people straining to put their experiences into logical sequences, when the real plot line was anything but straight. Think about it: how have you found work? What has been the mix of rational planning and unexpected magic?

One of the biggest assumptions in need of busting is that we don't matter and our influence will inevitably be small. Only when we learn to hold onto the awareness of our own value and vocation, can we free ourselves from the devaluing messages of the workplaces where we have been considered expendable. Only with that freedom can we set about finding or creating more worthy alternatives. Letting go of assumptions means waking up to our own role in creating the next possibility.

Co-create the Workplace You Want

It is natural for any system, whether it be human or chemical,
to attempt to quell a disturbance when it first appears.
But if the disturbance survives those first attempts at suppression
and remains lodged within the system, an iterative process begins.
The disturbance increases as different parts of the system get hold of it.
Finally, it becomes so amplified that it cannot be ignored.
This dynamic supports some current ideas that organizational change,
even in large systems, can be created by a small group
of committed individuals or champions.

MARGARET WHEATLEY, *LEADERSHIP AND THE NEW SCIENCE*

Be gentle as doves and wise as serpents.

JESUS OF NAZARETH

So far, we have been talking about choosing your next steps. Whatever you choose, though, you can count on its being imperfect. And so this chapter is about promoting healthy change and expanding your maneuvering room, moment by moment, in the course of doing your work. There are a thousand ways to do this, all of them difficult as well as rewarding. You can be an idea person, an ethics watchdog, a team builder, a supporter of the underdog, a redesigner of systems for getting things done, a prospector for new products or services. The term "co-creation" is used here to indicate that whatever you do is collaborative and evolutionary. Making significant changes at work is almost never a solo act.

There is an intimate connection between strategies to promote change in a workplace and strategies to protect and advance your own position. Both require a measure of clarity about personal power, both in a psychological sense and organizationally. Starting to think about change-agentry means thinking about how much we really believe in win/win, how we assess the trustworthiness of co-workers, how resilient we believe humans and organizations to be and where the leverage is in a given situation. This discussion will assume that every workplace has its own mix of communicators and backstabbers and its own set of organizational forces operating both for and against cooperative change. Yes, it's a jungle out there. But a jungle holds thousands of peaceable creatures as well as predators. It's home to stable communities. It thrives on diversity. Its relationships are characterized by massive interdependence. Survival requires a wider set of skills than competition alone.

The first step in co-creating the workplace you want is sinking roots in a job to achieve a solid understanding of the organization's mission, the agendas of those you work for and the degree of maneuvering room you have (both officially and unofficially). Just as all politics is local, all career strategy is interpersonal. It's about how you handle each assignment, meeting, memo, task list or chance encounter. Career self-defense and self-promotion are as necessary as ever. At the same time, they're an arena for putting forth the image of yourself for which you want to be known: your preferred balance of working solo and collaborating; cooperation and competition; directedness and acceptance; flexibility and limit-setting. These are the dilemmas in which strategy and values intersect. Where do you want to go? How do you want to get there? What is your position on Gandhi's famous principle that ends and means must harmonize? What factors do you pay attention to when you're assessing the potential for change, and the barriers?

Organizational dynamics are complex. But having a conscious, halfway sophisticated perspective on how an organization works is a marvelous advantage for surviving in one, to say nothing of making it a vehicle for the expression of your own values. Workplaces can be understood on many levels. Politics and cultural forces, financial and performance incentive structures, information flows and unconscious dynamics — experience tells us they are all in there helping to determine where the stepping stones lie on our paths.

For those with a reasonable tolerance for organizational complexity, one of the most welcomed forms of innovation and culture change is to help others navigate through it. You can do this as a mentor. You can do this as an information resource. You can do this as a resolver of conflicts and a problem-solving helper. Rick Sparks, a technical program manager for the software firm Dialogic in California, became an informal but recognized internal mediator after longstanding interest and self-education. The message he put out to co-workers was simply, "If you feel like you're in a Dilbert cartoon, come see me."

One of the most powerful kinds of workplace innovation is expanding the definition of the job you presently hold, whatever its level. For example, Nashville judge Penny Harrington presides over the nation's first county-wide environmental court, a role for which she volunteered after her colleagues had gone out of their way to distance themselves from the idea. This began a pattern Harrington has repeated successfully several times since: "taking on something everyone else hated, and realizing I knew what to do to make it work."

The season Harrington ran for the bench, a community groundswell was building for a special civil court that could address the backlog of building code violations in the city and surrounding countryside. A county "environmental" court, modeled on a successful citywide one in Memphis, would hear cases ranging from landlord-tenant disputes to illegal disposal of motor oil to Harrington's favorite, that of a man who could not seem to keep his 20 roosters properly caged.

In her first three years of running the court just a few days a month, Harrington saw tangible changes. Lawyers grew more willing to take on local environmental cases. Building inspectors said they got more cooperation from landlords. This feedback encouraged her to launch a second special docket, this time on domestic violence, with similar success. Largely due to the publicity, Harrington feels, "Women are saying for the first time, 'I don't have to take this. The courts will protect me.'"

"It's mostly a matter of being creative and noticing what the needs are," she advises. Of course, it doesn't hurt that Harrington has worked extensively on political campaigns and has been a lobbyist for a statewide environmental coalition. She readily admits: "I am no political neophyte."

At times, what starts out as a routine step to improve performance can lead to an entirely new emphasis or line of work. Richard Paradis and his fellow engineers in the US Navy found this out after a meeting in which they were directed by upper management to wrestle with a question: Why is it that we have such good regulations on paper for environmentally sound building construction, but we're not really doing it at its full potential? Out of that discussion came a Green Buildings program which began with a model renovation in the Navy's Virginia headquarters. Other projects followed. Guidelines, specifications and training materials arose from these. Soon the Navy was serving as a resource on greener buildings for the other military services and the federal government as a whole, and Paradis found himself representing the program.

"Intrapreneurship" is not just an option for those in the inner circles. In fact, often it's the new people who have the greatest chance at redefining their jobs. This is illustrated by the story of Annette Szumaski, who joined a large Washington law firm as a paralegal. Within a year, she had her superiors' blessing to create a new position as the firm's first environmental site inspector.

Her proposal filled a troublesome gap for her employer, whose business concentrated in environmental insurance litigation. Many of its cases involved long-standing, poorly documented claims of illegal practices, some with serious health effects. Private investigators hired from outside didn't always understand the environmental issues or the firm's needs. With a varied background that included technical writing and a period as a Pentagon analyst, Szumaski provided an intriguing combination of technical and political sensitivity.

For years, the fantasy of law school had danced before her eyes — but not with quite enough life to inspire commitment. She trained as a legal assistant to get her feet wet and intuitively looked for "an opportunity a little out of the ordinary." Szumaski was hired into the support staff to travel, conduct research, organize information, write reports and juggle all these demands. Her workload soon grew to include research into the history of contaminated sites. On her second research trip, Szumaski brought back information that was critical to victory for the firm's client. She also developed a fascination with environmental law and a conviction that "we have to clean up these sites, and we have to get the responsible parties to pay."

With the encouragement of the partner who had hired her, Szumaski carefully drafted a proposal for a new job description. Two committees fine-tuned it. One of their greatest concerns was where to put the position in the chain of command. She remained part of the support staff, but functioned independently.

Szumaski's story shows that it's possible to create fundamentally new positions, even in fields as highly structured as the law. "This process was evolutionary," she says. "I didn't try to change things overnight. It was happening, and I helped give it form." And the job, in turn, gave form to her next step, into law school.

As these cases show, the opportunities to make a difference in an organization do not correspond in any simple way to the formal power you may have. Your status, budget and job description are sources of power, but they don't necessarily outweigh the more subtle things like your working relationships, access to information, reputation and support system or the unpredictable shifts in markets and regulations which determine what your supervisors may be worried about.

Co-creating your workplace can also take the form of co-creating your field of work. For example, in the world of green building and design, thousands of professionals are engaged in a big, open-source experiment to test materials and concepts, create new business models and market to a new demographic, while holding onto their jobs and businesses and bringing in projects on time, within budget.

Of course, your maneuvering room for innovation increases when you happen to have a budget, a staff and some amount of a mandate. Even people who are nominally in charge may have trouble moving things in the direction they choose. But they certainly have wider options. And, in these times of flux, top jobs can be some of the highest-turnover positions around. In industry, government and the non-profit sector, the rule book of leadership is being rewritten by people at every organizational level.

Hazel O'Leary, the Clinton Administration's Secretary of Energy, earned one senator's nomination for a "Nobel Prize for guts in government" by admitting that military had performed radiation experiments on human subjects and endorsing the idea that the government owed victims and their families compensation. O'Leary also outlawed technospeak in the department; knocked down the bulletproof glass that surrounded her office area; replaced photos of missiles with others of wind farms and solar panels; froze contractor salaries and set standards for cost containment; started a large-scale project to declassify documents; and hired whistle-blowers and grassroots critics to positions of responsibility. Today she is on the speaking circuit talking about ways to create organizations that can handle change, starting with giving status and resources to people with diverging views. "When I first came to DOE, every other person I met was a nuclear engineer named Jim. You have to have different kinds of people sitting around the table or it simply won't work."

One of the limiting assumptions that may inhibit a change initiative is that consulting with stakeholders like customers, shareholders, employees and communities will get in the way of making decisions. In particular, it is unquestioned wisdom in some business circles that shareholders only want to see profits maximized. But when they're consulted, their views are actually more complex, and in many cases, they are perfectly capable of a longer-range vision. Even for a CEO, though, there is a risk in testing those boundaries. But consider the positive experiment carried out by Bill Hanley, chief executive officer of the largest publicly held military company to convert to civilian production. Galileo Electro-Optics, a 500-person high-tech firm in Sturbridge, Massachusetts, used to make night vision systems for the military. Period. Now the company uses variations on the same core technology to produce dozens of products: sensors on photocopy machines, medical and dental diagnostic equipment. An engineer who worked his way up through the manufacturing ranks at Corning Glass, Hanley says, "I can tell people on the shop floor honestly that I know their jobs, because I've done just about all their jobs."

Hanley is demanding as well as empowering. "What I run is a benign dictatorship," he admits, "because that's what it takes to turn an organization around." All these leaders I've highlighted here have risen in surprising settings — in the midst of highly resistant organizations or with no structure at all. All these leaders have walked in with a set of assumptions about what is possible that might have been considered naive and have proceeded, with extraordinary effort, to realize the possibility.

Hanley's story challenges one article of faith about the capacity of corporations to change. It is commonly held that the CEO of a publicly held corporation is powerless to do anything but maximize short-term profits for shareholders who are clamoring for their dollars. This is sometimes true, especially when the investors are pension funds with inflexible investment guidelines. But in 1985, when military contracting was booming and Galileo was entirely dependent on that single customer, Hanley made a long-shot pitch to his board of directors:

> This isn't going to last. Either the world is going to get more peaceful, or the world isn't going to last. We have to find other ways of earning a living here. It's going to take some adjustment in the short term, but it will put us in a lot better position in the long term.

Some board members left; others were attracted; and the company has maintained a stable population of investors who are willing to wait for the payoff, financially and otherwise.

Transformative leadership is showing its power in established industries.

And its role should not be overlooked in newer fields where people are discovering trade-offs and unanticipated consequences of their efforts, pointing to a need for activism to make a lot of good work better. For example, the groundswell of interest in Oriental medicine is giving millions of people alternatives to surgery, new avenues for pain management and an overall gentler set of tools for preventing disease and promoting wellness. At the same time, Oriental medicine's toolkit includes a large number of endangered plant and animal products such as rhinoceros horn, a fact that concerns a growing number of practitioners. In the *Acupuncture Alliance Forum*, acupuncturist Elizabeth Call wrestles with this issue:

> Since practitioners of Oriental Medicine believe that preventing or prolonging the onset of disease plays an important role in healthcare, it is clear that biodiversity plays a vital part in day-to-day clinical practice, from providing the source for herbal (and some allopathic) medicines, to protecting and inspiring humanity. We must expand our thinking from focusing on short-term issues to embrace solid solutions for the long-term survival of our profession, as well as our own species.
>
> The loss of biodiversity has emerged as one of the pressing environmental problems of our time. Addressing this problem requires a multi-disciplinary approach from within the sciences, as well as the inclusion of policy-makers and consumers in creating solutions...most importantly, though, it is the day-to-day behavior of all humans at home and at the workplace that will determine the ultimate survival of the human race (as well as our profession). Because the underlying philosophy of OM recognizes the interconnectedness of all things, we are in a good position to be role models for protecting biodiversity.

While it is customized for Oriental medicine practitioners, Call's prescription for change illustrates some general principles every profession and trade needs to consider. She urges fellow acupuncturists to:

- Become informed about the issues affecting your professional practice.
- Support labeling bills.
- Support the Acupuncture Alliance's boycott of formulas that contain or claim to contain endangered species.
- Challenge herb companies to provide documentation that their products are obtained legally and cultivated in a sustainable manner.

- Reduce, reuse and recycle whenever appropriate to alleviate pressure on natural resources.
- Devise ways to live and practice sustainably.

Sometimes, the innovation that makes all the difference is just to do one's job correctly, fairly and without corruption. This is a path of bravery in some workplaces where — in the words of Claire Booth Luce — "no good deed goes unpunished." While patient, thoughtful people can accomplish a great deal in their workplaces by the positive strategies of leadership and innovation, there are times when ethical resistance is legitimate and even necessary. The stories of whistle-blowers tend to arise as isolated cases. But their numbers are large, according to NASA whistle-blower Bill Bush, who lost his job and won it back through court action but was no longer assigned any work. Bush spent his idle hours on the payroll building a database of whistle-blowers in industry and government and accumulated 8,500 names.

The inventiveness of the mischief that rewards unpopular truth-telling in the workplace is well known. A 1987 survey by Donald Soeken, a Washington area social worker serving whistle-blowers, and his wife Karen, a statistician, showed that 84 percent of those who worked in private industry had been fired. In government, 75 percent were demoted. Any individual who stands up to an organization on issues of credibility and ethics can expect a period of extended challenge and stress, often culminating in a career change. The average time it took for whistle-blowers in this survey to resolve their legal cases was three to five years.[1]

The experience of whistle-blowing and related forms of public protest will change your life. A year-long investigation by the *Houston Chronicle* of the nuclear industry and its whistle-blowers revealed that most of them were forced into a career change. However, some of those changes end up as highly positive steps, as lawyer Billie Garde can affirm. Years ago, as a temporary worker in the census bureau in Muskogee, Oklahoma, Garde reported her boss for sexual harassment. He was investigated, indicted and convicted of more serious improprieties, including conspiracy to defraud the government. The experience led Garde to go to law school, and she now specializes in the legal defense of whistle-blowers for a Houston law firm. In the short run, the episode was devastating. In the long run, however, it forced her to break through to a new level of strength. She says frankly:

My previous life was lost. I didn't have anything to go back to. I had worked closely with a public interest law firm in pursuing my case. Then they hired me as an investigator. As I got stronger, I got interested in a legal career. I think that's because I saw that I was good at pointing out corruption and advocating for the truth. In the process, I became a different person.

Now, working with whistle-blowers who feel that their lives are falling apart, I say, "Let's review this. You lost your job. But it was in a corrupt organization that treated you like dirt. You lost your so-called friends. They ran away when your life got rough, so you didn't have much for friends anyway. What you lost was your illusions. What you do next is up to you."

If you think you see serious fraud, abuse or illegality around you, take time to document what you see and shore up your support system, before you make a move to disclose your concerns. Attorney Robert Backus, who works with whistle-blowers in the nuclear power industry, advises, "Keep careful records. First, they're going to say it's outside your area of concern. Then they're going to say it's not significant. You have to show why the issue is an issue." Consult the Government Accountability Project's manual, *Courage Without Martyrdom*, prepared by a team of experienced lawyers and counselors. Don't be shy about asking questions just because things seem more strange than they could possibly be.[2] In the words of one healthcare professional who was thinking of reporting possible research fraud, "I kept thinking, 'They couldn't be so transparent. They couldn't have gone so far.' The stunning part is how flagrant, how amateurish, it all seems."

As the need for whistle-blowers is better understood and the practice more common, state laws increasingly lay out their legal rights. The website of Public Employees for Environmental Responsibility, another support organization, tracks and ranks existing legal protections in each state. They vary widely. In spite of the challenges and the inconsistency of legal protection, however, 84 percent of the whistle-blowers who responded to the Soekens' survey said they would do the same thing again in the same circumstances. And an estimated 25 percent of whistle-blowers eventually see direct results from their action in the form of changes within the organization, and many others have a less direct impact in bringing about needed reforms. The sagas of Enron, Worldcomm,

NASA and the CIA would be very different without the courage of inside professionals willing to speak out when major companies and agencies lose their accountability.

Many whistle-blowers experience a double whammy: resistance and sometimes harassment by the employer and reluctance on the part of other employers to risk hiring them. But this is a taboo that can be broken, and many people reading this book can help. Anyone who has hiring power, even for a tiny department, can play a role. What is needed is the equivalent of an Underground Railroad — a commitment on the part of courageous employers to welcome courageous employees and reach out a strong hand to assist people who have told the truth at high cost.

This leads to the subject of organizational self-defense. The legal protections and social support systems which exist today for whistle-blowers have been built over decades, through tenacious and bitter battling, by whistle-blowers themselves and by activists, attorneys, legislators and helping professionals who see these people as frontline defenders of democratic institutions. The same is true for labor and workplace law.

Court battles and appeals to regulatory agencies both tend to be nasty, brutish and long. Their payoff can be high, morally as well as financially, but so can the investment that is required. While whistle-blower protection law was greatly expanded in the 1990s, its enforcement in recent years at the federal level has been limited.

At the same time, grassroots rebellions within organizations are becoming less and less surprising. For all the forces holding bad situations in place, there can be equal and opposite forces for innovation. Even changes that are not enough by themselves may bring unforeseeable ripple effects. Even the most toxic, unconscious, inconsistent, driven, nasty, neurotic organizations are still made up of human beings with at least a glimmer of desire for a better way to spend their days.

Sometimes an informed gamble pays off. At other times, wisdom dictates a conservative strategy. For example, according to organizational consultant Peter Block, it pays to be cautious when you're new or in an untested situation; when you or the organization are recovering from major change; when the survival of the organization (or your job) is threatened; and when you're in a zero-trust environment.

We have been talking about promoting change. Before proceeding further, it's worthwhile to consider the fact that revolutions through the ages have brought with them nasty surprises in terms of unexpected consequences. What principles might guide change agentry in a flexible and truly adaptive spirit? Here are a few to consider.

1. Accountability: identifying specific goals and people on whose behalf you're working (at least in your own mind, and preferably in your discussions with others who are affected), so that you get beyond ideology and have some concrete standards for evaluating your impact. When you take action on other people's behalf, make sure they know and support what you're doing.

2. Disclosure: being as open about your values and goals as you can in a situation, recognizing that there are limits to this but finding ways to build trust carefully over time and getting a grip on chronic secretiveness.

3. Start with an inside job. If you're pushing other people to deal with their "stuff," best deal with yours. How have your opinions on the issue been formed? Who have you tried to please over the years by the positions you've taken? It's easiest to see the issue through others' eyes — which you'll be called upon to do in countless ways — if you have some appreciation of your own blinders.

4. Responsibility. Taking risks to make change does not exempt you from responsibilities of your day-to-day job and working relationships. If you take an extra initiative, do so with grace and acceptance of the ways it may change your life. Having an agenda in an organization means carrying an added weight and setting yourself apart. Nobody is necessarily going to respond to your initiatives on your terms or timetable. Yours is the responsibility for meeting other people more than halfway, making the case and giving colleagues the resources to be helpful. This, in turn, requires tapping your own support system off the job for recharging and keeping perspective.

5. Follow-through and ongoing relationship. In Joanna Macy's words, "You can't change what you can't touch." Many of the best change agents root themselves deeply in the community they are trying to influence.

Investment analyst Linda Descano sums up these principles:

> If you're going to think of yourself as an intrapreneur on any level — which is a great thing to do — first you have to really understand the

workplace and the culture. That lets you identify opportunities that are very much consistent with the corporate culture, preferably in areas that you have some responsibility for. If you work in the print shop, start there, don't start calling for a building lighting audit. If you work in the cafeteria or an office, start there. If your ideas lead you to want to develop something commercial, then you have to do more than recommend something and believe in it. You must have strong financial skills, put the time into management and make a sound business plan so you will have stronger access to capital. Use networking, talk to people for feedback and to hone your own understanding. We often get so comfortable with our own views that we forget there's a world out there. Don't engage in eco-imperialism with your ideas.

Innovation has its risks. It is important to know your rights in the workplace and — whether or not you are trying to change the way business is done in your organization — get in the habit of navigating defensively through your career. This includes:

- Requesting periodic written feedback on your work (through reviews and in between reviews) and showing your cooperation (in action and writing) when problems are identified.
- Documenting any grievances carefully and non-judgmentally before presenting them.
- Keeping a professional portfolio of accomplishments, acknowledgments and references.

Some of these risks will be with you, no matter how sophisticated a player you are. The fact is, they'll be with you whether or *not* you take initiatives for change. Gifford and Elizabeth Pinchot write in their classic guidebook, *Intrapreneuring*, the First Law of the Intrapreneur is, "Come to work every day willing to be fired." But we have all lived through enough instability to put this in perspective. Often, when taking a risk doesn't lead all the way to the hoped-for conclusion, it leads somewhere more interesting than previously imagined.

For example, Dan Ruben was a healthcare administrator with a giant HMO, Harvard Pilgrim, for years. He had been involved with a program to help households reduce resource consumption by forming "Eco-Teams," and he realized that the same basic vision and strategy could apply to his company. "We had a lot of opportunities for environmental improvement, and I suspected that they would carry significant benefits for the bottom line," he said. Ruben wrote a proposal to create a job for himself as Environmental Affairs Coordinator for the Harvard Pilgrim system of 70 buildings, with 10,000 employees, serving over a million members. Tying the proposal carefully to the HMO's mission — improving neighborhood health — he started with a broad scan of opportunities, from water conservation to beach cleanups to employee environmental projects. The company president OK'd the proposal and directed Ruben to focus on saving paper, the most visible change for most of the workforce. Ruben recommended a company intranet, which was implemented. He achieved a redesign of the organization's major publication, its physician directory, reducing an unbelievable 110,000,000 printed pages per year to a mere 69,000,000. He spent the year 1997 evaluating the company's practices and making recommendations for savings. The process brought him widespread recognition. "It was such a high," he reflects. "About every two weeks, somebody would ask me to give a talk, write an article, join a board. I did it all. It was a joy."

Ruben's efforts saved Harvard Pilgrim hundreds of thousands of dollars. But that was not enough to prevent the organization from going into a tailspin for unrelated reasons. And he knew the days of joy were numbered. "When you're an HMO [Health Maintenance Organization] and laying off doctors, it's hard to hang onto your environmental function, no matter how much money it's saving." He was laid off, then invited back a year later, but not in his environmental role. Working as a project manager once again, he soon made a decision: to finish out his contract and then move into the environmental field. "Even if I end up taking a pay cut — which isn't guaranteed, but it's a possibility — the experience at Harvard Pilgrim made it abundantly clear where I need to move," he says. "What's more, it provided a bridge."

In the years since then, he has discovered an entrepreneurial flair in connection with greening more and more ambitious organizations, including a stint with a project to improve the environmental performance of the 2004 Democratic convention. Today he runs a business called Boston Eco-Tours, devoted to environmentally advanced practices in the city's convention and visitors' centers.

At the same time, there are situations that are less challenging than they appear. Howard Newman, a Los Angeles engineer and pacifist, did not feel comfortable working on weapons projects. He took a direct approach, typing at the bottom of his résumé "no war work." As a result, he has had a satisfying career in industries from toys to healthcare. Newman has never been out of work as a result of his position. But he did struggle, in the beginning, wondering what the path would be like.

During that struggle, Newman did a little interview project. He tells this story:

> I figured that the real experts on life's trade-offs would be people who had lived a long time and could look back, so I started talking to all the old people I could find. I asked them what they were happy about and what they regretted in their lives. I had conversations with 50 or 60 people. And with one exception — just one — they all said what they regretted were the risks they had not taken. Mistakes, failures, struggles — all those they had made peace with. Their lasting regrets were the risks, and the opportunities, they had missed.

A model blend of the entrepreneur and the intrapreneur is Matt De La Housaye, who took himself from Florida to Sweden to earn a master's degree in environmental economics at the University of Lund. Like many recent graduates, he and his closest friends found that their starter jobs didn't draw a whole lot on their educational background. But before long, he and two other fellow graduates were all bringing European environmental management ideas back to the US – one running a company that markets anaerobic digesters as an energy source; one working with industry on life-cycle management of products like computers that need proper recycling; and Matt as Project Manager for a district energy initiative called Eco-Grid in the little city of Hudson, NY, a job he was able to help create in this innovative startup.

It was his fourth job after graduate school, and the one where he decided to go for broke. "I wrote a list of goals at the beginning of 2006, and it started with 'renewable energy development.' That was my self-appointed title and I accomplished that, but realized there was something missing. The next year, on the list, I wrote "*successful*" renewable energy development.' At first, I had been happy just playing the game. Then I realized I needed to aim a little higher." Here is how he describes his blend of strategy and surrender:

> I've attached myself to very creative and entrepreneurial individuals in a number of cases. People who are originating things and have big visions – good for work, but also fun to be around. I've placed myself as the person who tries to

carry through on these people's ideas. I choose people first on trust. I do a lot of the evaluation by intuition, and I think I've learned different things from each person. Some people are really good at starting things, some are good at finishing. Some people articulate the vision, some keep the books." In part, you're discerning the capabilities of the person you are working for, but you are also looking at your own life. A year ago, I was splitting my life between New York City and Hudson, and hedging my bets, and that was going nowhere, so I said it's time to choose and follow through with one of these big ideas, so I made my commitment. Whether it worked or not, I reached the point of wanting to commit to one thing and ride it out. I chose this place because I felt there was a niche for me."

A constant networker, De La Housaye says he loves the big office environment but has mysteriously been attracted to tiny startups. So he brings together others like him for citywide "Green Drinks" events – the equivalent of a big office party for people with a lot of little offices. His morale comes from his motivation: "I have a handful of big goals and I just keep going toward them." He helped EcoGrid, as a startup, to acquire its first $100,000 for a feasibility study. Then, sensing that a more diverse set of contacts and income streams would give him stability, he said yes to a second opportunity in the same city. He was hired part-time by Advanced Recycling Technology, a recycler of hazardous materials on the global market, to help with research. He stepped onto that path and quickly gravitated to business development, creating a niche and only then realizing he had said yes to a job without any title. But it didn't matter. He had learned how to be an adaptive business generalist and create his own role.

To be a co-creator of your career means gauging risks, building a safety net and figuring out ways to land on your feet. If you have taken seriously the principles of creating a vibrant support system, stabilizing your life and letting your steps be guided by emerging needs around you, then you will master the art of co-creating your career — in your present workplace or the one that comes next.

APPENDIX 1

A Note to Career Counselors: Gatekeepers of a Positive Future

B*lown Sideways Through Life* is Claudia Shear's manic performance piece about being one step away from Bag Lady and learning to live there. For years Shear has been a waitress, proofreader, movie extra, receptionist in a whorehouse and many other things, all of which she is seriously overqualified for. Vaguely sensing that she was not of this world in the way employers like us to be, she sought out undemanding gigs where she didn't have to dress up, and could eat and read on the job to her heart's content. Then one day she looked at herself and realized she was a very well-read 200 pounds. "Writing this book is my 65th job," she admits. And it's the first one that she went after with some sense of her own potential.

Life-work counseling is coming into its own as a profession because a lot of people are seriously weary of being blown sideways and because the choices are more complex than ever, ethically and strategically. While the shock waves of corporate and governmental restructuring have intimidated some of us some of the time, they have also shaken much of the workforce out of passivity. Changes upon changes have driven home the idea that, in the words of Boston counselor Cliff Hakim, "we are all self-employed."

Whether they are in jobs or business ventures, whether non-profit or for-profit or government or some hybrid, working people have to be entrepreneurial today as never before. They have to self-define, self-motivate, self-promote and self-defend. They have to find ways of going about these things that are consistent enough with their values that they can look at themselves in the mirror at the end of the day. In these times, it is more important than ever for our clients to bring their whole selves into the quest for work and the doing of it. More important for us, too, if we are going to be any help to them.

This means we all have to grapple with a set of questions that were less critical to our profession in times when the options for our clients were more fixed. These are questions about the work that's out there and the capacities our clients are able to bring to it. Is altruism the opposite of realism, or is there a convergence taking place between values and pragmatism? Are "environmental careers" and "socially responsible business" and "community service" destined forever to be niches for idealists, or are there deepening connections between these worlds and the economy as a whole? And what is the appropriate role for career counselors as gatekeepers of possibility, who help our clients weigh risks and opportunities? What is *our* social responsibility when it comes to helping clients explore theirs? These questions are not going to go away, and our ability to deal with them directly can only help our clients muster courage for their own exploration.

In an era when both the future of work and the future of life on Earth are radically uncertain, our clients are faced with deeper levels of choice our profession has historically had to address — not just choices about their own opportunities, but about their responsibilities and potential for influence in the world. We must help them to hone their perceptiveness and critical thinking, so that they can carefully evaluate what's available now. We must also help them to name and sometimes bring into being what's important to them. Above all, we must help them to be brave.

There is a need for a new psychology of career development, one that is inseparable from the psychological and spiritual evolution of the individual and the culture. This approach takes aptitudes and skills into consideration but focuses on values and meanings — and, in particular, gives legitimacy to social and environmental values that are the wellspring of the human being's ability to care about his/her world. It amounts to recontextualizing every aspect of our lives, taking seriously that we are embedded within a cultural history and a living planet. For our clients and for ourselves, understanding our values and visions means knowing what we love enough to work hard for. It can be a source of a new level of resourcefulness in dealing with the stresses of any work situation, because it means shifting from "risk-management" to "opportunity-seizing" mode.

Aspiring to neutrality means risking irrelevance. At the same time, clearly, we cannot expect our own concerns and sensibilities to be mirrored by clients, or our own evaluation of the opportunities that make a difference to be a guideline for anyone but us. Somehow, we need to find a professional stance that is not value-neutral, but is not driven by a partisan or personal agenda either. The best language I've been able to come up with is Robert Lifton's "disciplined subjectivity."

Several primary influences have shaped this model:

- Developmental psychologists, such as Robert Kegan and the researchers at Wellesley College's Stone Center, who have pointed out the importance of relationship as a context for growth (not just specific relationships, but the awareness of oneself as related, which is not as obvious as it may seem).
- The literatures of athletic peak performance and accelerated learning, which both rely on strong personal vision coupled with structured training and frequent feedback for achieving behavioral goals.
- Multiple intelligence theory as articulated by Howard Gardiner and his colleagues at Harvard, reminding us how diverse and personalized people's learning styles are.
- Insights from the fields of general systems theory and organizational learning, as applied to social and organizational change, popularized by such practitioners as Joanna Macy and Peter Senge.

The guiding principle in this approach is supporting the client's *self* determination, but doing so with the clear awareness that the self is bigger than the ego and wiser than momentary impulse. I work as a guide to help people invent working lives that maximize contribution, and minimize harm, in their own eyes. I agree with many of my colleagues that it is not the counselor's place to suggest conclusions, only to frame the exploration and provide a container for dealing with the complexity, difficulty and full promise of the available options. This requires asking more questions and uncovering unexpected possibilities.

My approach flips one common assumption on its head: that before taking strong stands in the bigger world, humans must grow strong as individuals. Instead, I focus on the ways that we develop our strengths by engaging with our surroundings, speaking our truths, stretching ourselves. Moreover, any definition of mental health, development and well-being must include the capacity to take responsibility for the impact of one's actions on individuals, social groups and the ecological fabric of life.

Along with a new clinical paradigm, we need an expanded tool kit and fresh knowledge about the world of work. If we're encouraging clients to be entrepreneurial, we need to know about entrepreneurial financing, business planning, self-employment insurance, zoning laws governing cottage industries and more. As we encourage our clients to favor socially and environmentally responsible employers, we need to understand where they are and how to evaluate them. If we're encouraging clients to be change agents, we need an in-depth, unromantic understanding of workplace rights and self-defense strategies. We need to know how to support clients when they take risks that bring repercussions — not only emotionally, but legally and strategically.

I suggest three ways to work with the principles outlined in this book. The first is to focus on facilitating the client's discovery of the social environmental contexts that are important in his/her life. Second is to facilitate the client's discovery of the power to make a difference and draw on peer support in doing so. In fact, I prefer to use the book with committed groups rather than individuals one at a time. The third essential principle is to participate in the exploration with the client as a full human being, not a detached counselor-figure, owning our own biases and wishes and then letting them go.

No profession that is beyond its infancy has the luxury of staying value-neutral. Medical people have standards of health that they do their best to bring into patients' awareness and behavior. Psychologists have to hold out a vision of mental health, and their work is a complex interplay between their definition and their clients'. Career counselors, too, must grapple with a normative struggle revolving around the question, What is a successful career? Is it solely a matter of the client's personal preference? How do societal values figure in the conversation?

Arguably, helping clients take a broader, longer view can also support their financial and vocational self-interest. Employers that short-change ethics in their products and public positioning often do the same with their employees. Complicating the process with more questions is demanding, for us as well as for our clients — but isn't it ultimately easier for our clients to deal with comparative risks and values at the front end of a decision about a job or business opportunity, rather than later, when they're shoulder deep in the enterprise?

By now, at least, you have seen my reasons for believing that values ought to be regarded as the primary driver in career choices and that the social and environmental dimensions of values are among the most interesting areas of focus. After all, in the words of South African novelist Nadine Gordimer, a life divorced from any sense of social responsibility is a very lonely life. That is just one reason why it is in our clients' longer-term self-interest to rise to the challenges of the era — and in our interest to help them.

Making a Living
and a Difference Internationally

In the old town square in Prague on a business/pleasure trip some years ago, the human meaning of globalization started to come home to me. I walked out of a café and was pleasantly disoriented to hear the pipes and drums of an Andean band. I followed the sound and came upon a circle of Japanese and Western European tourists swaying to the Latin rhythms. Billboards advertised Apple and Sony and Toshiba against the backdrop of stunning thousand-year-old towers. That moment made it clear: there is hardly anyplace on Earth that isn't in touch with everyplace, for good or ill or both. Mobility across borders is a given in our lives, whether we are migrant farm workers or global product managers or itinerant musicians.

It was easy to feel part of one big, exuberant world — if I didn't think too hard. But neither the café nor the music nor most of the consumer products in circulation were in the reach of ordinary residents of the city. Most of them were too focused on making ends meet, to take part in this lighthearted moment.

One of my reasons for being in Prague was to write about Western environmental consultants who were helping devise ways of reducing the country's air and water pollution crises, a story I had earlier covered in Central America and in India. And through that story, I was becoming more aware of the limits of any help when it is brought by outsiders who in real ways have more political and economic power than the recipients.

Globalization represents a breakdown of boundaries and a potentially explosive upsurge of interconnections. It is a constant unfolding of opportunities to create something new out of the interplay of traditions, institutions, economies and ideas. William Irwin Thompson, one of planetary culture's real enthusiasts, describes his life this way, "When I go into the kitchen and cook...I cook what you could call, using a musical metaphor, planetary fusion. Mexican nachos with Indonesian sambal sate mixed in with the beans, then topped off with a cheese from Switzerland. And music is the right metaphor for what I see going on with planetary culture. Traditions from all over the world are jiving and giving us everything from Moroccan rock to Parisian rap."

But globalization is also a fiercely fought economic and geopolitical system with winners and losers — fragile cultures overrun by others that are more aggressive militarily or economically, to cite an obvious example. That is partly because of the differences in strengths and advantages of the players and partly because of the enormous unknowns. At each border between peoples, countries and cultures, there is an opportunity for enormous creativity, and for damage. The outcomes depend on how the relationships are negotiated and on what each player is willing to invest and risk.

Wendell Berry, a Kentucky farmer, poet and essayist, has long celebrated the local and decried the global. You can only take responsibility for what you love, he says, and you can only love what you can know in a deep and direct way. "Properly speaking, global thinking is impossible," Berry cautions, "and those who have practiced it have tended to be tyrants." In his view, environmental and social conscience only comes alive when people can see the impacts of their choices, directly and emotionally: an eroded gully, a population at risk, an assembly plant closing. However, you can live in a place all your life and hide out psychologically, declining to pay attention to the land and the river and the cultures around you. Or you can visit a new place and find your heart opening as it never did back home.

Futurist Hazel Henderson points out six different processes of globalization, reflecting both danger and potential: globalization of technology and production; work, employment and migration; finance, information and debt; military weapons and arms races; human impacts on the biosphere; and culture and consumption patterns. Each of these trends points to a cluster of career areas in which people can find good work, such as:

- International information services, including translation, editing, marketing of both print and online services
- International law, paralegal work and legal research
- Global finance and information services (working for the financial giants, or the emerging financial industries of the developing world, or for the social investment movement or for an information service that might level the playing field in your area of interest)

- Refugee resettlement, advocacy, social services and international human rights
- Community and economic development
- Technical and process innovation to help weapons companies diversify and make arms exporting a less seductive path
- Technology marketing and transfer, including the development of affordable ways to meet basic human needs like irrigation and vaccination
- Consumer marketing of socially responsible, fair-traded products
- Real ecotourism and natural resource protection
- Cultural outreach and connecting, from international museum partnerships to avant-garde jazz import-export businesses

That Prague moment of mine was 15 years ago. Power relations among nations and regions and cultural groups have shifted since then, sometimes growing more subtle and sometimes more confrontational. Transnational corporations have demonstrated their ability to abuse power in ecological issues from GMOs to the privatization of water. They have also pioneered social ventures and public interest investments on a substantial scale, including Unilever's work to bring useful consumer basics (laundry soap, blue jeans) into very low-income communities in ways that supported cottage industries and appropriate franchise businesses. Working in transnational corporations, at the point of social impact — for example, on sourcing or community relations — is an attractive strategy for making a good living and a difference, when the company genuinely supports the high-ground path.

Geopolitically, my home country has grown isolated in many respects. And yet it is still a wellspring of social innovation and a launching pad for the socially responsible business movement; it is one of the strongest bases for the non-profit sector globally and a place with much good to share. We in the US may be the advance guard for addressing a set of ethical questions that apply much more widely — questions about how we handle economic privilege and values conflicts between nations and peoples, while finding legitimacy in an international career that is geared toward positive impact.

Carrying an expanded work ethic into a global career requires making your own assessment of each new situation. As Sabrina Birner, an energy conservation consultant who worked in Thailand, reflected, "You can't automatically apply the same standards in Bangkok that you would in Harvard Square. But you can make a serious assessment of both current realities and the potential for change." That means listening to the strongest players and the most vulnerable ones, getting excited about your potential contribution, yet unromantic about the potential downside. It means following as well as leading. It means constant questioning. And so this section ends with an extra measure of questions for you to tape to the wall, near the place where you keep your passport.

1. Where are you going, literally and symbolically?
2. What are you leaving behind?
3. Who will be affected by the work you might do?
4. Will the outcome of your work involve winners and losers?
5. Who will lose if you win? (Try to get beyond the abstract and imagine particular people and places.)
6. Are there actions or attitudes you could take on the job that would make it more of a win-win situation?
7. How certain are you of your power to produce a fair outcome, even if you can imagine one?
8. What do you know about the people and cultures of the place where you are considering working?
9. How have you chosen your sources of information about them?
10. Are there others you should consult for a balanced view?
11. What technologies and tools will you use in your work?
12. How will they affect the quality of life and the balance of power you and your co-workers have with the local population?
13. What do you want to believe about this place?
14. What attracts you most?
15. What scares you?
16. What do you know about the ecology and natural history of the place?
17. What can you do while you're there, to help protect or restore a healthy ecology, including taking responsibility for your style of living?
18. What peoples have held this place sacred?
19. How will your actions affect their lives, communities and cultures?
20. What can you do to learn more about the indigenous people and bring their message, whatever it is, back to your home community?
21. Will you displace or compete with local people who might otherwise be doing "your" work?

22. What local social or political groups will you be most closely allied with in this place?
23. Could this put you into conflict with any others?
24. Are there ways you might *realistically* serve as a peacemaker in the community where you'll be?
25. Are there ways you could do the good things mentioned above without actually transplanting yourself?
26. What kinds of power will you bring into the situation?
27. How will it compare to the power of the people you'll be working with, supervising and reporting to?
28. Are there ways you can make this power balance fairer and more productive?
29. Is this trip or move a rite of passage for you in any way?
30. How has it come to have this meaning?
31. Are there ways you could achieve the same symbolic goal with accomplishments or adventures closer to home?
32. How do you define your commitment to your home community?
33. Whatever choice you make, how can you maximize the positive impact of your international work and minimize the negative?

RESOURCES

Essential Career Development Resources

American Psychological Association, Public Interest Directorate. *Career Guidebook for Students of Color*. Order from publicinteres@apa.org

Cameron, Julia. *The Artist's Way*.

Covey, Steven R. *The 8th Habit: From Effectiveness to Greatness*. Simon & Schuster.

Diaz, Ande. *The Harvard College Guide to Careers in Public Service*. Harvard University Office of Career Services, 1995.

Jarow, Rick. *The Alchemy of Abundance: The Art and Science of Manifestation*. Sounds True, 2005, meditation CD included, $19.95.

Jarow, Rick. *Creating the Work You Love: Courage, Commitment, and Career*. Inner Traditions, 1995.

Kidder, Rushworth. *How Good People Make Tough Choices*.

Kushell, Jennifer. *The Young Entrepreneur's Edge*. Random House, 1999.

Nolo Press Employee Rights Resource Center: nolo.com

Occupational Outlook Handbook: bls.gov/oco/

Parker, Yana. *The Damn Good Resume Guide*: damngood.com

Sanders, Tim. *Love is the Killer App*.

Sinetar, Marsha. *Do What You Love, the Money Will Follow*.

Stone, Douglas, Bruce Patton, Sheila Heen and Roger Fisher. *Difficult Conversations: How to Discuss What Matters Most*. Penguin, 1999.

Vault career guides focusing on high-level business/industry (e.g., consulting, biotech, Capitol Hill, finance) with message boards on particular employers: vault.com

Vogt, Peter. *Measure Your Soft Skill Smarts*. Monster Career Trak.

Wall Street Journal's Career Journal Online: careerjournal.com

Industry and Interest Portals

Animal care and rights: Fitzsimmons, Paula. *105 Careers for Animal Lovers: For People Who Want to Express Their Passion for Animals Through Meaningful Careers*: pjpublications.com

Environmental careers: ecojobs.com; environmentalcareer.com

Environmental health: Association of Environmental Health Academic Programs: aehap.org

Environmental Restoration, Society of: ser.org

Environmental non-profits, small. See Orion Grassroots Network: oriononline .org/pages/ogn/vieworg.cfm

Federal government jobs: usajobs.opm.gov and studentjobs.gov

Foundations and philanthropy: fdncenter.org

Geographic information systems/mapping: gis.com

Hake, Katherine. Very broad, quirky, informative career portal website: khake .com.

Hoovers company reports: hoovers.com

Human resources/training: American Society for Training and Development: astd.org

Land protection: Land Trust Alliance: lta.org

Law: thellcn.com

Library science: ala.org/ala/education

Mediation: mediate.com

Ministry: exploreministry.org

Non-profit careers: idealist.org; nptimes.com

Nutrition: nutritionsociety.org

Planning: planning.org

Social Workers, National Association of: socialworkers.org

Sustainable business: sustainablebusiness.com (Green Dream Jobs)

Water management: Water Infrastructure Network win-water.org

ENDNOTES

Introduction

1. North American Regional Consultation on Sustainable Livelihoods. "Principles of Sustainable Livelihoods." *Earth Ethics*. Spring 1995, pp. 12–13.
2. Laurent Daloz-Parks, Cheryl Keen, James P. Keen and Sharon Parks-Daloz. *Common Fire: Lives of Commitment in a Complex World*. Beacon Press, 1996.
3. "Beyond the Green Corporation." *Business Week*. January 23, 2007.
4. Joshua Humphrey et al. *2005 Report on SRI Trends in the US: A 10-Year Review*. Social Investment Forum, 2005.
5. Ray Anderson, Paul Anderson and Sherry Anderson. *The Cultural Creatives: How 50 Million People Are Changing the World*. Harmony Books, October 2000.
6. Arne Naess. "Self Realization." *Thinking Like a Mountain: Toward a Council of All Beings*. New Society Publishers, 1987.

Chapter 1

1. Global Reporting Initiative: globalreporting.org
2. *Non-profit Times* salary surveys at nptimes.org
3. Rosabeth Kanter. "From Spare Change to Real Change." *Harvard Business Review*. May 2000.
4. City of Tulsa press release at cityoftulsa.org/News/Climate5-15-07.asp
5. Thanks substantially to the work of Joel Makower, editor of the newsletter *Clean Edge*: cleanedge.com

Chapter 2

1. Rebecca J. Goldberg, Matthew S. Elliot and Rosamond L. Naylor. *Marine Aquaculture in the United States*. Report for the Pew Oceans Commission.
2. National Gardening Association website: garden.org

3. Center for a New American Dream website: newdream.org, summer 2007.
4. Statistics from the website of the Land Trust Alliance: lta.org; urban land trust information and resources available from E.F. Schumacher Society smallisbeautiful.org
5. A microcosm of eco-fashion is on view at Linda Loudermilk's website: linda loudermilk.com
6. Scott Graham. *Handle with Care: A Guide to Responsible Travel in Developing Countries*. Noble Press, 1991.

Chapter 3

1. American Medical Association. *Health Professions Career and Education Directory, 2006–2007.*
2. Health Care Without Harm: noharm.org
3. GradPsych Career Center: gradpsych.apags.org/career.html

Chapter 4

1. Ron Fox. *Lawful Pursuit: Careers in Public Interest Law*. American Bar Association, 1995. Center for Professional Development in the Law. Tel. (781) 639-2322 Fax (781) 639-2322 (call first): ronaldwfox.com

Step 1

1. Phil Jackson. *Sacred Hoops*. Delacorte, 1995.
2. Duane Elgin. *Voluntary Simplicity: How to Create a Life That Is Outwardly Simple, Inwardly Rich*. Morrow, 1981, revised 1993.
3. Sam Deep and Lyle Sussman. *What to Ask When You Don't Know What to Say: 555 Powerful Questions to Use for Getting Your Way at Work*. Addison-Wesley, 1993.
4. Thomas Berry. *The Great Work*. Crown, 1999.
5. Stephanie Armour. "Managers Not Prepared for Workplace Violence." *USA Today*, July 19, 2007.
6. Joanna Macy and Molly Young Brown. *Coming Back to Life: Practices to Reconnect Ourselves, Our World*. New Society Publishers, 2001.
7. Jim Autry. *Love and Profit*. Avon, 1991, p. 32.

Step 3

1. Barbara Sher with Annie Gottlieb. *Wishcraft*. Ballantine, 1979.

2. Cliff Hakim. *We Are All Self-Employed*. Berrett-Kohler, 1994.

3. Carol Goldberg and Dawn-Marie Driscoll. *Members of the Club*. Beacon Press, 1993.

4. Jeff Reid. "Networking Overtime." *Utne Reader*, Sept/Oct 1993.

5. Bill Walker. "Green Like Me." *Greenpeace Magazine*, May/June 1991.

6. Carolyn Myss. *Anatomy of the Spirit: Seven Stages of Power and Healing*. Crown, 1996.

7. Rick Jarow. *Creating the Work You Love: Courage, Commitment and Career*. Destiny Books, 1995.

8. Jerry Mander. *In the Absence of the Sacred: On the Failure of Technology and the Survival of the Indian Nations*. Sierra Club Books, 1991.

Step 6

1. ThinkExist.com Quotations Online June 1, 2007; July 13, 2007: einstein/quotes/martha_graham/

2. Barbara Winter. *Making a Living Without a Job*. Bantam, 1994.

3. Michael Porter. *Competitive Advantage: Creating and Sustaining Superior Performance*. Harvard Business School Press, 1998

Step 7

1. David Dorsey. "A New Spirituality of Work: Interview with Richard Barrett." *Fast Company*, July 31, 1998.

2. Sharon Welch. *A Feminist Ethic of Risk*. Fortress, 1990.

3. Natalie Goldberg. *Long, Quiet Highway: Waking Up in America*. Bantam, 1993.

4. Graduation Pledge Alliance: graduationpledge.org

Step 9

1. Adam Bryant. "Talking Management with: John Cleese — Soldier of Convention or Agent of Change?; A Rebuff to the Ministry of Silly Bosses." *New York Times*, February 7, 1999, section 3, p. 1.

Step 10

1. Donald and Karen Soeken. "A Survey of Whistleblowers, Their Stressors and Coping Mechanisms." Self-published report, 1987, available from 15702 Tasa Place, Laurel MD.

2. Tom Devine. *Courage Without Martyrdom.* Government Accountability
Project, 1612 K St. NY, Suite 1100, Washington, DC 20006, 202-408-0034.

INDEX

ABOUT THE AUTHOR

MELISSA EVERETT has made a career of helping people — and communities — figure out their "right livelihood." As a career counselor and trainer of counselors, she has worked with populations that range from businesspeople to divinity students. Since the first publication of *Making a Living While Making a Difference* in 1995, she has been developing a distinctive framework for vocational empowerment that has drawn interest in the U.S., Asia, Europe and Latin America. From her own "day jobs" in nonprofit management, she has helped to finance and guide several environmental education organizations. Today, as Executive Director of Sustainable Hudson Valley, she works to redirect local and county economic development in support of environmental and community goals. Her Ph.D. is from Erasmus University in the Netherlands.

If you have enjoyed *Making a Living While Making a Difference,*
you might also enjoy other

BOOKS TO BUILD A NEW SOCIETY

Our books provide positive solutions for people who want to
make a difference. We specialize in:

Sustainable Living • Ecological Design and Planning

Natural Building & Appropriate Technology

Environment and Justice • Conscientious Commerce

Progressive Leadership • Resistance and Community • Nonviolence

Educational and Parenting Resources

New Society Publishers

ENVIRONMENTAL BENEFITS STATEMENT

New Society Publishers has chosen to produce this book on recycled paper made
with 100% post consumer waste, processed chlorine free, and old growth free.

For every 5,000 books printed, New Society saves the following resources:[1]

35	Trees
3,174	Pounds of Solid Waste
3,492	Gallons of Water
4,555	Kilowatt Hours of Electricity
5,770	Pounds of Greenhouse Gases
25	Pounds of HAPs, VOCs, and AOX Combined
9	Cubic Yards of Landfill Space

[1]Environmental benefits are calculated based on research done by the Environmental Defense
Fund and other members of the Paper Task Force who study the environmental impacts of the
paper industry.

For a full list of NSP's titles, please call 1-800-567-6772 *or check out our web site at:*

www.newsociety.com

NEW SOCIETY PUBLISHERS